Ellie Roland

MASTERWORK ®

ESSENTIAL MESSAGES FROM GOD'S SERVANTS

Oct. 5. 2011

Lessons from

SPIRITUAL LEADERSHIP

by Henry & Richard Blackaby

HEAVEN

by Randy Alcorn

FALL 2011

LifeWay

Biblical Solutions for Life

Lessons by Henry & Richard Blackaby are condensed from *Spiritual Leadership* (Nashville, B&H Publishing Group, 2001). Used by permission. All rights reserved.

Lessons by Randy Alcorn are condensed from *Heaven* (Tyndale House Publishers, copyright © 2004 by Eternal Perspective Ministries). Used by permission. All rights reserved.

MasterWork: Essential Messages from God's Servants (ISSN 1542-703X, Item 005075042) is published quarterly by LifeWay Christian Resources of the Southern Baptist Convention, One LifeWay Plaza, Nashville, Tennessee 37234; Thom S. Rainer, President. © Copyright 2011, LifeWay Christian Resources of the Southern Baptist Convention.

For ordering or inquiries, visit *www.lifeway.com*, or write LifeWay Church Resources Customer Service, One LifeWay Plaza, Nashville, TN 37234-0113. For subscriptions or subscription address changes, e-mail *subscribe@lifeway.com*, fax (615) 251-5818, or write to the above address. For bulk shipments mailed quarterly to one address, e-mail *orderentry@lifeway.com*, fax (615) 251-5933, or write to the above address.

Printed in the United States of America.

Cover photo credit: Stephen Swintek/Getty Images

All rights reserved.

MIKE LIVINGSTONE
Content Editor

ALAN RAUGHTON
Lead Adult Ministry Specialist

DAVID APPLE
Adult Ministry Specialist

DWAYNE MCCRARY
Editorial Project Leader

Send questions/comments to
Content Editor, *MasterWork*
One LifeWay Plaza
Nashville, TN 37234-0175
Or make comments on the web at
www.lifeway.com

Management Personnel

Bret Robbe, *Director*
Leadership and Adult Publishing

Ken Braddy, Ron Keck, Debbie Johnson
Managing Directors
Leadership and Adult Publishing

David Francis, *Director, Sunday School*

Bill Craig, *Director*
Leadership and Adult Ministry

Gary Hauk, *Director Publishing*
LifeWay Church Resources

ACKNOWLEDGMENTS. We believe that the Bible has God for its author; salvation for its end; and truth, without any mixture of error, for its matter and that all Scripture is totally true and trustworthy. The 2000 statement o *The Baptist Faith and Message* is our doctrinal guideline.

TABLE OF
CONTENTS

STAYING FIT ... SPIRITUALLY.

We talk a lot of the importance of staying physically fit, but what about the health of our spirits? Connect, Grow, Serve, Go is a call to evaluate your present spiritual condition and discover ways to improve your spiritual health. Packed into each biblical concept—Connect, Grow, Serve, Go—is a simple way you can move forward, not remain stagnant. Best of all, these tools will stand the test of time—no "fad" diets here. They will help you become spiritually healthy—and stay that way.

❤ CONNECT
WITH AN OPEN HEART
MARK 12:29-31

urges you to worship, pray, fellowship, and relate to others in positive relationships at work, in the home, and in other settings. Spiritual fitness results when you connect with God, with others, and with your church family.

♫ GROW
IN BODY, MIND, & SPIRIT
ROMANS 12:2

refers to learning and understanding more about God and His expectations of His people, which comes through Bible study. You grow by applying that knowledge to your everyday living.

✋ SERVE
WITH WILLING HANDS
1 PETER 4:10-11

describes the work you do inside your church. Your church is full of ministry and service opportunities. You serve by using your spiritual gifts, skills, and passions to glorify God. All of us must work together for the church to function as God intended.

👣 GO
WITH READY FEET
MATTHEW 28:19-20

moves you outside the church and into the community and the world. Evangelism and missions are ways to go into your community and the world in the name of Jesus Christ. It might be uncomfortable at first, but you will experience firsthand the difference Christ can make through you.

CONNECT, GROW, SERVE, GO must impact you before it can permeate your circle of friends, your Bible study group, and then your church as a whole. But balance is the key! We must be actively participating in all four areas if we want to be spiritually healthy. All Go and no Connect with God or other believers results in powerless activity and wears you out. A steady diet of Grow without the action of Serve or Go leads to unhealthy spiritual obesity and laziness. We need a balanced spiritual diet to remain fit and able to serve God in the ways for which He has gifted us.

The "Leader Guide" after each lesson in MasterWork will offer suggestions to help you, your Bible study leader, and your Bible study group to Connect, Grow, Serve, or Go. Look for these CONNECT ❤, GROW ♫, SERVE ✋, or GO 👣 icons in this and other adult study resources from LifeWay Christian Resources to help you check and maintain your spiritual balance and health.

WELCOME TO MASTERWORK

MasterWork provides challenging, Christ-centered Bible study material along with a modern perspective from some of today's most respected Christian leaders. Renowned authors draw learners to a deeper level of involvement through daily personal study, weekly group interaction, and key life messages. This resource features:

- Short daily studies to help both leader and learner prepare for each week's session
- Interspersed interactive personal learning activities in bold type to help draw points of application to reader's lives
- A two-page teaching plan following each lesson to help facilitators guide learners through lessons

MasterWork is easy to use and easy to lead. Both leader and learner read the same Scripture, study the same lesson, and answer the same discussion questions. When they come together, the teacher functions as a group facilitator, setting the pace and guiding students through a lively and spirited in-class session.

ADDITIONAL RESOURCES AVAILABLE

- *nExtra*—Exchange teaching ideas and discuss upcoming lessons with other MasterWork users. Join *nExtra,* a free virtual community for teachers using LifeWay's Adult Sunday School resources. Check it out at *www.lifeway.com/nextra.*
- **Biblical Illustrator Plus**—a quarterly CD-ROM edition of the print magazine, *Biblical Illustrator*. Each issue of BI Plus offers several well-researched articles that relate to the *MasterWork* lessons. For ordering information go to *www.lifeway.com/biblicalillustrator.*

ABOUT THE WRITERS

HENRY BLACKABY is one of the world's most popular speakers and writers. His *Experiencing God* study course has sold more than three million copies. He is president of Henry Blackaby Ministries.

RICHARD BLACKABY is president of the Canadian Southern Baptist Seminary in Cochrane, Alberta.

MARGARET DEMPSEY-COLSON wrote the personal learning activities and teaching plans for this study. Margaret teaches Sunday School at First Baptist Church, Marietta, Georgia.

SPIRITUAL LEADERSHIP

Secular and spiritual leaders may use similar methods, but there are dimensions to spiritual leadership not present in secular leadership. Spiritual leaders who simply follow secular methods may experience some degree of success, but they will not rise to the higher level of leadership possible for true spiritual leaders. This study will distinguish between general leadership principles and spiritual leadership principles.

Only when we understand leadership in light of God's calling on our lives will we be equipped to lead effectively. According to the Bible, God is not necessarily looking for leaders, at least not in the sense we generally think of leaders. He is looking for servants (Isa. 59:16; Ezek. 22:30). When God finds men and women willing to be molded into His servants, the possibilities are limitless. People are looking for someone to lead them into God's purposes God's way. They need leaders who truly believe God will do what He says. People will follow spiritual leaders who understand God's agenda and who know how to move them on to it.

As you participate in this study, we pray you will accept the challenge to be that man or woman God is seeking to use. We hope you will experience the incredible joy and satisfaction of knowing God is using your life as His instrument to build His kingdom and to change your world.

—HENRY & RICHARD BLACKABY

The Leader's Challenge

DAY ONE

Leadership: The Challenge

Leadership. Everyone experiences it, or the lack of it, in their daily lives. Those called to lead can find doing so a daunting task. Those expected to follow can experience frustration when their leader is unable to lead and their organization seems to be going nowhere. Struggling leaders may agonize in the knowledge that others resent them and blame them for their organizations' failures. Countless discouraged leaders would probably quit their jobs today, but they need the income. Besides, they fear the same problems would engulf them in their new jobs. Discouraged, Christian leaders carry the added, albeit misguided, burden that they are failing not only their people but their Lord. They feel guilty because they lack the faith to move their organization forward yet the same fears prevent them from leaving their leadership positions for jobs where they might be more successful. Is there any hope for the countless numbers of leaders who are not experiencing the fulfillment and reaching the potential God intended for them? If anything can revolutionize today's Christian leaders, it is when Christians understand God's design for spiritual leaders.

Leadership. Everyone experiences it, or the lack of it, in their daily lives.

What leaders have personally made an impact on you—either positively or negatively? In what ways? My friend Ellie: I want me now to be normal!

What leadership roles do you have? (Consider family, workplace, community, and church responsibilities.) _big Sister_
friend, student,

What is the greatest challenge you face in your leadership role?
To Stay Calm & positive.

The twenty-first century provides unprecedented opportunities for leaders to make a positive impact on their organizations. However, the new millennium also has brought unforeseen challenges to leaders. The digitalized nature of the twenty-first century has created increasing expectations among followers, and the unrelenting advance of technology has made communication both a blessing and a curse.

Past leaders had certain times in their day when they were inaccessible to people. During such times they could reflect on their situation and make decisions about their next course of action. Technology has made today's leaders constantly and instantly accessible to people. With such access, people often expect immediate responses from their leaders. Such pressure to make rapid decisions and to maintain steady communication can intimidate even the most zealous leader.

The rise of the Information Age has inundated leaders with new information that must be processed as rapidly as possible. Today's leaders are bombarded with books, articles, and seminars on leadership and management theory as well as data pertaining to their particular field of work. An exhausting parade of books claims that if busy executives will simply follow the proposed steps, they will be guaranteed success. Leaders wanting to improve their skills and expand their knowledge base have virtually limitless opportunities to enhance their leadership skills. But where does one begin? Which book does a leader read next? Which seminar is a must? Which management trend vociferously advocated now will be passé by next year? Such a bombardment of information, much of which is contradictory, can cause leaders to become cynical. It is no wonder so many leaders express the frustration that they are always hopelessly behind.

Our world craves good leaders. It would seem that effective leadership has become the panacea for every challenge society faces. Whether it's in politics, religion, business, education, or law, the universally expressed need is for leaders who will rise to meet the challenges that seem to overwhelm many of today's organizations. The problem is not a shortage of willing leaders. The problem is an increasingly skeptical view among followers as to whether these people can truly lead. Warren Bennis warned, "At the heart of America is a vacuum into which self-anointed saviors have rushed."[1] People know intuitively that claiming to be a leader or holding a leadership position does not make someone a leader. People are warily looking for leaders they can trust.

DAY TWO

Leadership: In the Church

The political scene is perhaps the most public arena where people have expressed their distrust in those who lead them. The business world cries out for leaders as fervently as the political world. Even the religious community has not escaped the leadership drought. Jesus Christ warned His followers about false prophets who would rise up to lead many astray (Matt. 24:11), but who could have anticipated the plethora of would-be spiritual leaders who have flooded the airwaves and descended upon churches with their books and their theories, clamoring for followers? It boggles the mind that destructive and delusional gurus such as Jim Jones and David Koresh could gain so many devoted followers. It is incomprehensible that well-educated people with lucrative jobs, upscale houses, and comfortable lifestyles have sold everything and abandoned their families, friends, and reputations to follow a self-declared messiah who assured them they would one day be taken away by UFOs! It is even more amazing that sincere people would

SCRIPTURE

"Many false prophets will rise up and deceive many" (Matt. 24:11, HCSB).

follow such delusional prophets to violent deaths for the sake of oblique causes. What motivates people to blindly follow these would-be messiahs? People are desperate for leaders who can make positive changes in their lives!

Society at large is displaying widespread and growing interest in spiritual issues. Amazingly, at a time of renewed societal interest in spiritual things, many churches and denominations are declining. According to George Barna, "the American church is dying due to a lack of strong leadership. In this time of unprecedented opportunity and plentiful resources, the church is actually losing influence. The primary reason is the lack of leadership. Nothing is more important than leadership."[2]

Immorality is an epidemic in the church. Pastors face issues today far more complex and divisive than ministers faced only a generation ago. In order to survive, churches are seeking leaders who can not only overcome the voluminous challenges churches are facing, but also attract new members and resources in order to finance an increasingly expensive organization. One thing seems certain: while many theological seminaries are enjoying healthy enrollments, denominational leaders are bemoaning the fact that their schools are graduating so few leaders. Although the leadership shortage is universally acknowledged, there is little consensus on how to discover and develop leaders. Seminary professors are bewildered that so few successful leaders are emerging from their graduating classes.

> "The American church is dying due to a lack of strong leadership."
> – George Barna

What are the greatest leadership needs of today's churches?

Why are there not more effective leaders in churches today?

DAY THREE

Leadership: Secular or Spiritual?

Is Christian leadership the same thing as secular leadership?

NoPe

This issue of leadership holds a deeper dimension for Christians: Is Christian leadership the same thing as secular leadership?

What do you think are some differences between secular and spiritual leadership? *One is for self Pleasure & the other is for Others!*

Modern bookstores have capitalized on the chronic thirst for leadership. They stock shelves and shelves with books on leadership and management. Leaders who have been successful in business, sports, politics, or any other field have written autobiographies detailing their success. The myriad of such books testifies to the large number of people eagerly scouring the pages hoping to find the secret to their own effectiveness as leaders in their respective fields. The question many Christian leaders face is whether the principles that make people successful leaders in sports or business are equally valid when applied to leadership issues in the kingdom of God. The pastor examines the leadership style of a successful football coach and wonders: Will these same principles work for me as I lead my church?

This raises a significant issue for Christian leaders: Do leadership principles found in secular writing and seminars apply to work done in God's kingdom?

How would you answer Blackaby's question in the paragraph above? What evidence do you have to support your opinion?

_____
_____
_____
_____
_____
_____
_____
_____
_____
_____

The current generation of Christian leaders has immersed itself in the popular leadership writings of its day. This acceptance of secular approaches by Christian leaders can be observed in numerous places. The shift in the traditional nomenclature from the pastor's study to the pastor's office is one consequence. In times past, churches focused on the Great Commission. Today's churches adopt mission statements. In earlier times, churches spoke of building fellowship. Contemporary Christian leaders build teams and lead their people through team-building exercises. Churches used to put church signs in front of their buildings in the hopes of attracting people to their services. Today's churches use state-of-the-art marketing principles to reach their communities. Pastors of large churches (and some not so large) are beginning to act more like CEOs than shepherds. The pastor's office is located in the Executive Suite, next to the boardroom where the leadership team meets. Is this adoption of secular leadership methodology a sorely needed improvement for churches? Or is it woefully inadequate? Is it a violation of biblical principles? Many church leaders claim these innovations have resulted in dramatic growth in their congregations, including a significant proportion of converts. Other Christian leaders decry such approaches as blatant theological and biblical compromise.

The trend toward a CEO model of ministry has changed the churches' evaluations of effective leadership. The pastor's ability is measured in terms of numbers of people, dollars, and buildings. The more of each, the more successful the pastor. The godliness of a minister may not be enough to satisfy a congregation looking to keep up with the church down the street. Likewise, Christian organizations seem willing to overlook

> Is this adoption of secular leadership methodology a sorely needed improvement for churches? Or is it woefully inadequate? Is it a violation of biblical principles?

significant character flaws, and even moral lapses, as long as their leader continues to produce.

The trend among many Christian leaders has been for an almost indiscriminate and uncritical acceptance of secular leadership theory without measuring it against the timeless precepts of Scripture. This study will look at contemporary leadership principles in light of scriptural truth. It will become clear that many of the "modern" leadership principles currently being espoused are, in fact, biblical principles that have been commanded by God throughout history. For example, secular writers on leadership are insisting on integrity as an essential characteristic for modern leaders. This is nothing new for Christians. The Bible has maintained that as a leadership standard for over two millennia.

Paradoxically, concurrent with the churches' discovery of popular leadership axioms, secular writers have been discovering the timeless truths of Christianity. Leadership experts are discovering that doing business in a Christian manner, regardless of whether one is a practicing Christian, is, quite simply, good for business. Earlier leadership theories assumed the best CEOs were larger-than-life, charismatic people who stood aloof from those they led, giving orders to be followed unquestioningly. In contrast, today's leadership gurus are writing books that appear almost Christian. Book titles such as *Jesus CEO, Management Lessons of Jesus, Servant Leadership, Love and Profit, Leading with Soul*, and *Encouraging the Heart* sound like they ought to be shelved in a Christian college, not in the office of a corporate CEO.

The Christian tenor of these books goes beyond their titles. It is common to read in secular leadership books that companies should make covenants with their people, that business leaders should love their people, that managers should be servant leaders, that leaders should show their feelings to their employees, that business leaders must have integrity, that leaders must tell the truth, and interestingly, that leaders must strive for a higher purpose than merely making a profit. These principles appear to be more in keeping with the Sermon on the Mount than with the Harvard Business School. Incredibly, as secular writers are embracing Christian teachings with the fervency of first-century Christians, Christian leaders are inadvertently jettisoning many of those same truths in an effort to become more contemporary!

Incredibly, as secular writers are embracing Christian teachings with the fervency of first-century Christians, Christian leaders are inadvertently jettisoning many of those same truths in an effort to become more contemporary!

DAY FOUR

God or King?

The willingness of God's people to barter their spiritual birthright for the benefit of contemporary secular thinking is not unique to this generation. During Samuel's time, the Israelites were a small, insignificant nation in the midst of international superpowers. They were content to have Samuel as their spiritual guide and God as their king. But as Samuel grew old, his ungodly sons abused their leadership positions. The Israelites compared themselves to neighboring nations and envied their powerful armies, their magnificent cities, and the glory of their monarchies. Rather than trusting in God to win their battles, to direct their economy, and to establish laws for their land, the Israelites wanted to be just like all the other nations with a king who would do this for them. They took their request to Samuel. In response, Samuel gave them God's appraisal of where this pursuit for a king would lead them (1 Sam. 8:10-22).

> **Read 1 Samuel 8:10-22 in your Bible. Summarize what Samuel said to the people about the consequences of choosing worldly leadership over divine leadership.** _____
>
> _____
> _____
> _____
>
> **Why do you think the Lord granted their request for a king?**
> _____
> _____
> _____
> _____

The world measured a kingdom's success by its grand palaces and magnificent armies. The glittering trappings of such monarchies dazzled the Israelites. But citizenship in such a kingdom came with a stiff price.

Sustaining a monarchy required oppressive taxes from its citizens. The Israelites wanted a mighty army, but a royal army would require even heavier taxation as well as a draft of young Israelite men for the king's purposes. A monarchy could not function without a legion of servants; this would require the people's children to be conscripted to serve the king. God could not have been more clear about the consequences of choosing worldly leadership over divine leadership. Yet the Israelites stubbornly persisted in their pleas, so God granted them a perfect specimen of a worldly leader. Saul was handsome and physically impressive—yet he was insecure and incredibly vain. He was decisive, sometimes making on-the-spot pronouncements—but many of these had to be rescinded later because they were foolhardy. He was a passionate man—but he was also prone to violent temper tantrums. Saul was a hands-on general—who spent the bulk of his time chasing after his own citizens. The Israelites clamored for a leader who would lead them by worldly principles. God gave them one, and the results were disastrous.

What went wrong? The problem was the Israelite's assumption that spiritual concerns, such as righteous living and obedience to God, belonged in the religious realm while the practical issues of doing battle with enemies, strengthening the economy, and unifying the country were secular matters. They forgot that God Himself had won their military victories, brought them prosperity, and created their nation. He was as active on the battlefield as He was in the worship service. When the Israelites separated spiritual concerns from political and economic issues, their nation was brought to its knees. Scripture indicates that it is a mistake to separate the spiritual world from the secular world.

Applying spiritual principles to business and political issues doesn't call for Baptist pastors to serve as military generals, nor does it require seminary professors to run the economy. God created people to be spiritual beings. Every person, Christian and non-Christian alike, is a spiritual person with spiritual needs. Employees, customers, and governing boards all have spiritual needs that God wants to meet through His servants in the workplace. God is also the author of human relationships. He has established laws in relationships that have not changed with the passing of time. To violate God-ordained relationship principles in the workplace is to invite disaster. Jesus Christ is the Lord of all believers whether they are at church or at work. The kingdom of God is, in fact, the rule of God in every

> The Israelites clamored for a leader who would lead them by worldly principles. God gave them one, and the results were disastrous.

> Jesus Christ is the Lord of all believers whether they are at church or at work.

area of life, including the church, home, workplace, and neighborhood. To ignore these truths when entering the business world or political arena is to do so at one's peril.

Society's problem is more than just a lack of leaders. Society's great deficit is that it does not have enough leaders who understand and practice Christian principles of leadership. Effective leaders are not enough. Hitler was an effective leader. The world needs people in business who know how to apply their faith in the boardroom as well as in the Bible study room. Jesus summed up this truth for every executive, politician, schoolteacher, lawyer, doctor, and parent, when He said: "But seek first his kingdom and his righteousness, and all these things will be given to you as well" (Matt. 6:33, niv).

~
SCRIPTURE

"But seek first the kingdom of God and His righteousness, and all these things will be provided for you" (Matt. 6:33, HCSB).

Is it possible to be successful in business or politics while seeking God's kingdom first? Explain your answer. _____

_____

_____

_____

_____

_____

_____

_____

_____

The world needs husbands and wives, mothers and fathers who know how to apply biblical promises in their homes rather than merely implementing advice from the latest self-help books.

Books such as *Loving Monday* by John Beckett, *It Is Easier to Succeed Than to Fail* by Truett Cathy of Chick-fil-A, and *Character Is the Issue: How People with Integrity Can Revolutionize America* by Governor Mike Huckabee of Arkansas provide examples of Christians who have successfully incorporated their Christianity into their business and politics. The business world has recognized these leaders and rewarded them for their leadership efforts. The world needs political leaders who seek their guidance from the Holy Spirit and not from the latest public opinion poll. The world needs religious leaders who are on God's agenda and not on their own. The world needs husbands and wives, mothers and fathers who know how to apply biblical promises in their homes rather than merely implementing advice from the latest self-help books.

DAY FIVE

Conclusion

Christian leaders who know God and who know how to lead in a Christian manner will be phenomenally more effective in their world than even the most skilled and qualified leaders who lead without God. Spiritual leadership is not restricted to pastors and missionaries. It is the responsibility of all Christians whom God wants to use to make a difference in their world. The challenge for today's leaders is to discern the difference between the latest leadership fads and timeless truths established by God. It is to this end that this book has been written. We hope it will encourage you to be the Christian God is calling you to be.

It is our sincere belief that the following passage applies to every Christian: "The eyes of the Lord move to and fro throughout the earth that He may strongly support those whose heart is completely His" (2 Chron. 16:9a).

What are some external evidences of a heart that is completely God's?_____

_____

Concepts for Consideration
- People know intuitively that claiming to be a leader or holding a leadership position does not make someone a leader.
- Is Christian leadership the same thing as secular leadership?
- Paradoxically, concurrent with the churches' discovery of popular leadership axioms, secular writers have been discovering the timeless truths of Christianity.
- The Israelites clamored for a leader who would lead them by worldly principles. God gave them one, and the results were disastrous.
- Christian leaders who know God and who know how to lead in a Christian manner will be phenomenally more effective in their world than even the most skilled and qualified leaders who lead without God.

Spiritual leadership is not restricted to pastors and missionaries. It is the responsibility of all Christians whom God wants to use to make a difference in their world.

SCRIPTURE

"The eyes of the LORD move to and fro throughout the earth that He may strongly support those whose heart is completely His" (2 Chron. 16:9a, NASB).

1. Warren Bennis, *Why Leaders Can't Lead* (San Francisco: Jossey Bass, 1989), 36.
2. George Barna, *Leaders on Leadership* (Ventura: Regal Books, 1997), 18.

LEADER GUIDE

Before the Session

1. Make one large poster for the classroom, titled "Spiritual Leadership." Beneath the title write six sub-titles: "The Leader's Challenge," "The Leader's Role," "The Leader's Preparation," "The Leader's Vision," "The Leader's Character," and "The Leader's Goal."

2. Enlist someone to be prepared to summarize 1 Samuel 8 to the class.

During the Session

1. Introduce the study by asking the rhetorical question: *Do you see yourself as a leader?* Direct learners' attention to the quote in the margin of page 17: "Spiritual leadership is not restricted to pastors and missionaries. It is the responsibility of all Christians whom God wants to use to make a difference in their world." In the study introduction on page 6, Blackaby states "God is not necessarily looking for leaders, at least not in the sense we generally think of leaders. He is looking for servants. When God finds men and women willing to be molded into His servants, the possibilities are limitless." State that all Christians have leadership opportunities—in the home, workplace, church, or community. Emphasize this study will help us to accept the challenge to be that man or woman God is seeking to use. Point to the poster and draw attention to the title for the study and the focus for each of the following six weeks. ◐

2. Summarize the first full paragraph on page 9. ("Our world craves good leaders.") While we crave good leaders, we know that holding a leadership position does not necessarily make someone a leader. Direct attention to the George Barna quote in the margin of page 10. Ask learners if they agree or disagree, and why.

3. Ask for responses to the first bolded question on page 10, *What are the greatest leadership needs of today's churches?* Ask: *Have the leadership needs of churches changed in the last fifty years? Explain.* Ask the second bolded question on page 10, *Why are there not more effective leaders in churches today?*

4. Use the material in Day Three to discuss the differences between secular leadership and spiritual leadership. Ask these questions: *Is Christian leadership the same thing as secular leadership? What are some differences? Can secular leadership principles apply to work done in God's kingdom? How do you see secular leadership principles being followed in the church today? Why are many secular writers embracing Christian leadership principles?*

5. State that when we abandon biblical principles and measure success according to secular thinking we are flirting with disaster. Call on the person enlisted earlier to summarize the events that unfolded in 1 Samuel 8. Discuss: *Why do you think the people wanted a king? Why did Samuel consider their request sinful?* (See v. 6.) Suggest that their request was motivated by a desire to conform to the pattern of other nations. Ask: *What would be the consequences of choosing worldly leadership over divine leadership?* (See vv. 10-22.) *Why do you think the Lord granted their request?* (See *mystudybible.com* for helpful notes on this passage.)

6. Ask a volunteer to read Matthew 6:33. Ask: *Can we seek first the kingdom of God and still be successful leaders in the world? Explain.* Emphasize that our calling as Christians not only takes precedence over our jobs; it can actually give direction to our careers. A Christian's calling will give meaning to every area of life. Ask: *What is your calling as a Christian?* ☊

7. Read the last three sentences on page 16 (beginning with "The world needs political leaders …."). Direct learners' attention again to the quote in the margin of page 17. Close in prayer, asking God to reveal to participants how they can become the spiritual leaders God wants them to be.

After the Session

Pray for and encourage class members in their various leadership roles, whether those leadership roles are in the church, workplace, home, or community. Strive to be a leader worthy of imitation.

The Leader's Role: What Leaders Do

DAY ONE

What Is Leadership?

"Leadership is one of the most observed and least understood phenomena on earth" asserts James MacGregor Burns.[1] Voluminous material is currently being published on the subject of leadership, yet there seems to be no simple, universally accepted understanding of what leaders do. Without clearly understanding their role, leaders are destined for failure.

Warren Bennis and Burt Nanus in their book, *Leaders: Strategies for Taking Charge,* report that they discovered over 850 different definitions of leadership.[2] No wonder today's leaders are unsure how they measure up. There are too many standards to meet! Each definition offered seeks to contribute a new insight to the understanding of leadership, and many of them do. The following is a sampling of the diversity of helpful definitions that have been offered:

- "Leadership is the process of persuasion or example by which an individual (or leadership team) induces a group to pursue objectives held by a leader or shared by the leader and his or her followers" (John W. Gardner, *On Leadership*).[3]
- "Leadership is influence, the ability of one person to influence others" (Oswald Sanders, *Spiritual Leadership*).[4]
- "The central task of leadership is influencing God's people toward God's purposes" (Robert Clinton, *The Making of a Leader*).[5]

facebook H

Each of these definitions helps bring focus upon the role of leaders. Some are secular definitions and, therefore, although they address general leadership principles, they do not take God and His purposes into account. In this study we will use the term "spiritual leadership." This is not to distinguish between leaders of religious organizations and business leaders guiding secular companies. It is to identify leaders who seek to lead God's way. To be a spiritual leader is just as essential in the marketplace as in the church.

Do you agree that being a spiritual leader is just as essential in the marketplace as in the church? Explain. *YES. both need strong but wisdom and knowledge.*

> To be a spiritual leader is just as essential in the marketplace as in the church.

John Gardner's definition employs the terms "persuasion" and "example" to indicate the means leaders should use to move people toward their objectives. This secular definition fails to take into account God's will and the guidance He gives to leaders. Secular leaders may lead people to achieve their goals, even goals held by their followers. But this is not the focus of spiritual leaders. Spiritual leadership involves more than merely achieving goals. People can accomplish all of their goals and still not be successful in God's kingdom.

Sanders, in his classic work *Spiritual Leadership*, suggests that leadership is influence. Sanders is exactly right in asserting that leaders who make no difference in their followers' lives are not actually leaders. Influence, however, may be too broad a term to describe adequately the act of leadership. While benefiting from the contribution of Sanders, today's leaders need help in knowing how to exert an influence that is according to God's will.

> People can accomplish all of their goals and still not be successful in God's kingdom.

Robert Clinton's definition encompasses the spiritual nature of leadership in that God's people are led toward God's purposes. Clinton wisely observes that God's purposes are the key to spiritual leadership—the dreams and visions of leaders are not. While we find this to be a helpful

> God's purposes are the key to spiritual leadership—the dreams and visions of leaders are not.

21

definition, we would like to add at least two dimensions to it. First, spiritual leaders can lead those who are not God's people as well as those who are. Christian leadership is not restricted to within church walls but is equally effective in the marketplace. Second, Clinton notes that leaders lead their people toward God's purposes. However, simply leading people toward an objective may not be adequate for a spiritual leader. Many pastors have left their churches after serving less than two years. They may argue that they moved their church forward, yet nothing of lasting significance was accomplished. But just as Moses was not released from his followers when they disobeyed God and began a 40-year hiatus in the wilderness, so true leaders stay with their people until they have successfully achieved God's purposes. Moses himself had remained faithful to God, yet God would not release him from his rebellious people.

What does Moses' perseverance with his followers—even in their disobedience—teach us about being a spiritual leader? *you*

Stink with your follow no matter what!

To abandon followers because they refuse to follow is to forsake the sacred calling of a leader. Spiritual leaders know they must give an account of their leadership to God; therefore, they are not satisfied merely moving toward the destination God has for them; they want to see God actually achieve His purposes through them for their generation.

A New Definition. There are a number of helpful definitions of leadership available, but we believe true spiritual leadership can be defined in one concise statement:

> *Spiritual leadership is moving people on to God's agenda.*

This is a brief definition, perhaps not as technically precise as some, but we believe it describes what is at the heart of being a spiritual leader. At least five truths are inherent in this definition, which we will examine over the next two days.

DAY TWO

The Spiritual Leader's Task, Part 1

Spiritual leadership is not identical to leadership in general. While spiritual leadership involves many of the same principles as general leadership, spiritual leadership has certain distinctive qualities that must be understood and practiced if spiritual leaders are to be successful. The following are the distinctive elements of spiritual leadership implied in our definition.

1. *The spiritual leader's task is to move people from where they are to where God wants them to be.* This is influence. Once spiritual leaders understand God's will, they make every effort to move their followers from following their own agendas to pursuing God's purposes. People who fail to move people on to God's agenda have not led. They may have exhorted, cajoled, pleaded, or bullied, but they will not have led unless their people have adjusted their lives to God's will. Our definition assumes that spiritual leaders use spiritual means to move or influence people as opposed to methods devoid of God. When spiritual leaders have done their jobs, the people around them have encountered God and obeyed His will.

The spiritual leader's task is to move people from where they are to where God wants them to be.

How is God using you to move people on to His agenda? *Show*
Emma & Erica not to be bad

2. *Spiritual leaders depend on the Holy Spirit.* Spiritual leaders work within a paradox, for God calls them to do something that, in fact, only God can do. Ultimately, spiritual leaders cannot produce spiritual change in people; only the Holy Spirit can accomplish this. Yet the Spirit often uses people to bring about spiritual growth in others. Moses dealt with this paradox when God commissioned him to go to Egypt to free the Israelites. God said, "'I have surely seen the affliction of My people who are in Egypt, and have given heed to their cry because of their taskmasters, for I am aware of their sufferings. So I have come down to deliver them from the power of the Egyptians, and to bring them up from that land to a good and spacious land…'" (Ex. 3:7-8). So far, this sounded fine to Moses. God was going to do something that

Spiritual leaders depend on the Holy Spirit.

only God could do. Then God added an unsettling instruction, "'Therefore, come now, and I will send you to Pharaoh, so that you may bring My people, the sons of Israel, out of Egypt'" (Ex. 3:10). That is the crux of spiritual leadership. Leaders seek to move people on to God's agenda, all the while being aware that only the Holy Spirit can ultimately accomplish the task.

3. Spiritual leaders are accountable to God. Spiritual leadership necessitates an acute sense of accountability. Just as a teacher has not taught until students have learned, leaders don't blame their followers when they don't do what they should do. Leaders don't make excuses. They assume their responsibility is to move people to do God's will. Until they do this, they have not yet fulfilled their role as leaders. True spiritual leadership is taking people from where they are to where God wants them to be.

> Spiritual leaders are accountable to God.

Read Exodus 3:11; 4:1,10,13. Describe each of Moses' four expressions of reluctance to be God's leader.

1. _He said who am I?_
2. _He said that they would dobt him_
3. _Said yes not good at speaking_
4. _Wanted someone else to do it_

How have you in the past been reluctant to be God's leader?

yes. Charter for this year.

DAY THREE

The Spiritual Leader's Task, Part 2

> Spiritual leaders can influence all people, not just God's people.

4. Spiritual leaders can influence all people, not just God's people. God is on mission at the local factory as well as at the local church. His agenda applies in the marketplace as well as the meeting place. Although spiritual leaders will generally move God's people to achieve God's purposes, God can also use them to exert significant godly influence upon unbelievers. The biblical account of Joseph is a case in point. God's plan was to spare the Egyptians from a devastating seven-year famine and, through the Egyptians, to provide food for other Middle Eastern people as well. Pharaoh was an unspiritual leader. He did not understand the message God was giving, so God sent Joseph to advise him. It was Joseph, a man of God, who was able to interpret God's warning and to mobilize the pagan nation to respond to God's activity. There may not be anything overtly spiritual about building grain storage bins or developing a food distribution system, but these activities were on God's agenda. God did not choose to use the religious experts of the day. Instead, He chose to make Himself known to an unbelieving society through a God-fearing government official.

How is God using you to accomplish His will among unbelievers? _by being nice & godly_

_____

_____

_____

5. *Spiritual leaders work from God's agenda.* The greatest obstacle to effective spiritual leadership is people pursuing their own agendas rather than seeking God's will. God is working throughout the world to achieve His purposes and to advance His kingdom. God's concern is not to advance leaders' dreams and goals or to build their kingdoms. His purpose is to turn His people away from their self-centeredness and their sinful desires and to draw them into a relationship with Himself. For example, when Jesus took Peter, James, and John with Him to the mount of transfiguration, God the Father had a specific will for His Son. The Father brought Moses and Elijah to encourage Jesus for the great work of redemption He was about to accomplish. So glorious and sacred was that moment that Jesus was transfigured and the glory of God radiated about Him. Peter and his companions, however, had been asleep. When they awoke and saw the magnificent scene unfolding, Peter spoke up: "'Master, it is good for us to be here; let us make three tabernacles: one for You, and one for Moses, and one for Elijah" (Luke 9:33). The moment Peter began talking, the vision was removed, and only Jesus remained visible. It's not clear what Peter's intention was, but it

Spiritual leaders work from God's agenda.

is obvious that Peter's agenda was not God's agenda. The Heavenly Father immediately rebuked Peter, saying, "This is My Son, My Chosen One; listen to Him!" (v. 35). Incredibly, Peter attempted to get Jesus, Moses, Elijah, James, and John to adjust their lives to his plan, instead of seeking to understand God's agenda and adjusting his own life accordingly.

Peter's mistake is all too prevalent among spiritual leaders. Too often, people assume that along with the role of leader comes the responsibility of determining what should be done. They develop aggressive goals. They dream grandiose dreams. They cast grand visions. Then they pray and ask God to join them in their agenda and to bless their efforts. That's not what spiritual leaders do. Spiritual leaders seek God's will, whether it is for their church or for their corporation, and then they marshal their people to pursue God's plan.

The key to spiritual leadership, then, is for spiritual leaders to understand God's will for them and for their organizations. Leaders then move people away from their own agendas and on to God's. It sounds simple enough, but the truth is that many Christian leaders fail to put this basic truth into practice. Too often leaders allow secular models of leadership to corrupt the straightforward model set forth by Jesus.

Briefly describe how Moses' life exemplified the five distinctive elements of spiritual leadership.

1. The spiritual leader's task is to move people from where they are to where God wants them to be (Ex. 3:7-8). *yes*

2. Spiritual leaders depend on the Holy Spirit (Ex. 3:12; 33:12-17).
Moses depended on ther

3. Spiritual leaders are accountable to God (Num. 20:12).
yup

4. Spiritual leaders can influence all people, not just God's people (Ex. 2:15-22). *yes.*

5. Spiritual leaders work from God's agenda (Heb. 11:24-26).

yup.

i dont get this...

bored.

DAY FOUR

Spiritual Leadership: Jesus as the Model

Even secular writers recognize Jesus as a compelling model of good leadership. Numerous scholars have attempted to explain Jesus' leadership style. Scholars have developed complete leadership systems and leadership training models based on what they discovered as they examined Jesus' methods of leadership. Jesus' life is so profound and so beyond our common experience that we must continually reexamine it, lest we assume Jesus operated merely by leadership theory that we value today.

Jesus did not develop a plan nor did He cast a vision. He sought His Father's will. Jesus had a vision for Himself and for His disciples, but the vision came from His Father. Some portray Jesus as a leader who first accepted the enormous assignment of redeeming a lost and corrupt world, and then was sent to figure out how to do it. This is clearly a misunderstanding of Jesus' ministry.

Some leadership development proponents observe that Jesus concentrated primarily on training twelve followers; they conclude this model of leadership must be the pattern for all spiritual leaders. While not depreciating the value of leadership development or the significance of small group dynamics, leaders would be remiss to infer that the methodology Jesus adopted is the key to spiritual leadership. It is not. The key to Jesus' leadership was the relationship He had with His Father.

> Even secular writers recognize Jesus as a compelling model of good leadership.

> The key to Jesus' leadership was the relationship He had with His Father.

In what ways does your relationship with God impact your leadership? *you can but we cant on him to h if is you!*

_____

_____

_____

Jesus developed His relationship with God the Father as well as with people (Luke 2:52). Since He knew the Father, Jesus recognized His voice and understood His will. Because He knew the Father's will, Jesus did not allow people's opinions to sidetrack Him from His mission (Mark 1:37-38).

The temptations in the wilderness were Satan's attempts to prevent Jesus from obeying the Father (Matt. 4; Luke 4:1-13). Satan approached Jesus with a proposition: "So, your assignment is to bring salvation to the people of the earth. That's a big job. Let me help you. Turn these stones into bread, because if you feed the people they will follow you." Jesus refused, so Satan offered another suggestion: "Cast yourself from the top of the temple. When the angels save you, everyone will see the miracle and they'll know you are God's Son. Then they will follow you." Again, Jesus refused. Satan offered a final alternative: "Jesus, there's no point in fighting over the dominion of this earth. Bow down and worship me, and I will hand over all the people to you. Then you won't have to do battle with me, and you can avoid the cross. Crucifixion is despicable and is totally unnecessary in order for you to accomplish your goals." Once again, Jesus refused to take any shortcuts in carrying out His Father's will. This would not be the last time Jesus would have to resist such temptations (John 6:15; Matt. 12:38; 27:40).

Satan's overt temptations follow a familiar pattern. First, there's an easier way, with a lower personal cost. Second, God's way is not necessarily the only option in achieving the desired goals. But there was also a more subtle temptation at work here. Satan sought to persuade Jesus that saving the world was His job, so He should develop His own plan to get the job done. Satan was offering what appeared to be shortcuts to God's will, but shortcuts that carried with them devastating consequences. Jesus, however, was never required to develop ministry goals or action plans. He was sent to follow the Father's plan, to the letter.

Even choosing the Twelve was not Jesus' idea but His Father's. Scripture says Jesus spent an entire night praying before He chose His disciples (Luke 6:12-13). This was a critical juncture in Jesus' ministry; perhaps it took most of the night to understand clearly the Father's plan for the Twelve.

On the night of His crucifixion, Jesus once again indicated that the Father had chosen His disciples. In what is commonly referred to as Jesus' High Priestly Prayer, He gave an account to His Father for all that the Father had given Him. "I have revealed you to those whom you gave me out of the world. They were yours; you gave them to me and they have obeyed your word. Now they know that everything you have given me comes from you" (John 17:6-7, niv).

This passage indicates clearly that Jesus did not choose 12 disciples as a matter of strategy. Nor was there any formula in the number 12. Jesus did not calculate that 12 was the optimum number for His ministry. Jesus had 12 disciples because that is how many His Father gave Him. Would Jesus have chosen Judas if He were simply implementing a discipleship strategy to multiply His efforts? Judas was included because he was given to Jesus as a part of God the Father's redemptive plan.

According to Jesus, even the teaching He gave His disciples came from the Father (John 14:10; 15:15; 17:8). If these 12 men were to develop into the leaders God wanted them to be, the disciples would need the Father's teaching. Jesus understood that He was to facilitate the relationship between His disciples and His Father. His task was to bring His disciples face to face with the Father so they could develop the same intimate relationship with Him that Jesus enjoyed (John 14:8-11).

Jesus came to fulfill His Father's plan of salvation. He spent each day looking to see what the Father would reveal about His will. When He observed the Father at work, Jesus adjusted His life to join Him.

Describe a situation when you saw God at work and adjusted your life to join Him.

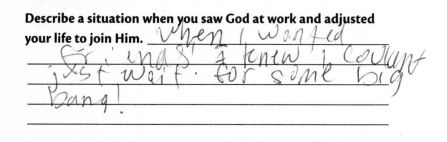

When Jesus entered the large city of Jericho, with masses of people crowding along the streets trying to catch a glimpse of Him, Jesus did not set the agenda for that day. He did not strategize: "This is the last time I will pass through this great city. What can I do to make the greatest impact on the crowd and see the most people accept the gospel?" Instead, Jesus spotted the diminutive Zaccheus in a tree. Out of the intimate relationship Jesus had with His Father, He recognized the Father's activity in the despised tax collector's life, and He invited Zaccheus to spend time with Him (Luke 19:1-10). Had Jesus entered the city planning to have lunch with the most notorious sinner of that region? No. He had simply watched for the first sign of the Father's activity. Once He saw where the Father was working, Jesus immediately knew the agenda for His ministry. Likewise, He trained His disciples to watch for God's activity rather than to set their own agendas.

Even in the most difficult assignments, including the cross, Jesus accepted His Father's will unwaveringly. Jesus left His future, as well as His Second Coming, for the Father to determine. Jesus characterized His entire ministry with these words: "By myself I can do nothing" (John 5:30, niv).

Jesus characterized His entire ministry with these words: "By myself I can do nothing" (John 5:30, NIV).

❈

DAY FIVE

Conclusion

Jesus has established the model for Christian leaders. It is not found in His "methodology." Rather, it is seen in His absolute obedience to the Father's will. Current leadership theory suggests good leaders are also good followers, and this is particularly true of spiritual leaders. Spiritual leaders understand that God is their leader. If Jesus provides the model for spiritual leadership, then the key is not for leaders to develop visions and to set the direction for their organizations. The key is to obey and to preserve everything the Father reveals to them of His will. Ultimately, the Father is the leader. God has the vision of what He wants to do. God does not ask leaders to dream big dreams for Him or to solve the problems that confront them. He asks leaders to walk with Him so intimately that, when He reveals what is on His agenda, they will immediately adjust their lives to His will and the results will bring glory to God. This is not the model many religious leaders, let alone business leaders, follow today, but it encompasses what biblical leadership is all about.

Is it possible for God to guide leaders so that their actions, and even their words, are not theirs, but His? Yes. Does God have an agenda for what He wants to see happen in the workplace? He does. Our prayer should be that which Jesus instructed His disciples to pray: "Your kingdom come, your will be done, on earth as it is in heaven" (Matt. 6:10, niv). If Christians around the world were to suddenly renounce their personal agendas, their life goals and their aspirations and begin responding in radical obedience to everything God showed them, the world would be turned upside down. How do we know? Because that's what first century Christians did, and the world is still talking about it.

> If Christians around the world were to suddenly renounce their personal agendas, their life goals and their aspirations and begin responding in radical obedience to everything God showed them, the world would be turned upside down.

Are you following God's agenda or your own? _____

_____

_____

_____

Concepts for Consideration
- People can accomplish all of their goals and still not be successful in God's kingdom.
- Spiritual leaders do not try to satisfy the goals and ambitions of the people they lead but those of the God they serve.
- Christian leadership is not restricted to within church walls but is equally effective in the marketplace.
- Spiritual leaders know they must give an account of their leadership to God; therefore, they are not satisfied merely moving toward the destination God has for them; they want to see God actually achieve His purposes through them for their generation.
- Spiritual leadership is moving people on to God's agenda.
- God's concern is not to advance leaders' dreams and goals or to build their kingdoms.
- Spiritual leaders seek God's will, whether it is for their church or for their corporation, and then they marshal their people to pursue God's plan.

1. James MacGregor Burns, *Leadership* (New York: Harper Torchbooks, 1978), 2.
2. Warren Bennis and Burt Nanus, *Leaders: Strategies for Taking Charge* (New York: HarperCollins, 1997), 4.
3. John Gardner, *On Leadership* (New York: The Free Press, 1990), 1.
4. Oswald Sanders, *Spiritual Leadership* (Chicago: Moody Press, 1967; reprint ed., 1994), 31.
5. Robert Clinton, *The Making of a Leader* (Colorado Springs: NavPress, 1988), 203.

Pray about your role as a Sunday School leader. Are you accepting opportunities in that role to move people on to God's agenda? Seek God's will for the class as a whole as well as for individuals in the class.

LEADER GUIDE

Before the Session

Make a sentence strip with Blackaby's definition of spiritual leadership: "Spiritual leadership is moving people on to God's agenda."

During the Session

1. State that this is the second week in a six-week study of leadership. As time allows, summarize the key points of the September 4 lesson. On the poster you made for last week's lesson, point to the title of today's lesson: "The Leader's Role." State that a good starting point in becoming the leaders God wants us to be is having a right understanding of what leadership is. Read the three definitions offered by John W. Gardner, Oswald Sanders and Robert Clinton on page 20. Using the material of Day One, discuss the pros and cons of each definition. Point to the sentence strip and ask participants to read Blackaby's definition of spiritual leadership aloud and in unison.

2. Explain that Moses was an exemplary spiritual leader. Before he said *yes* to God, however, he expressed reluctance to be a leader. Call on volunteers to read Exodus 3:11; 4:1,10,13 and identify Moses' expressions of reluctance. Ask participants to share personal experiences of reluctance to be God's leader.

3. Continue the discussion of Moses by highlighting how his life exemplified each of the five distinctive elements of spiritual leadership explained by Blackaby: (1) The spiritual leader's task is to move people from where they are to where God wants them to be (Ex. 3:7-8); (2) Spiritual leaders depend on the Holy Spirit (Ex. 3:12; 33:12-17); (3) Spiritual leaders are accountable to God (Num. 20:12); (4) Spiritual leaders can influence all people, not just God's people (Ex. 2:15-22); and (5) Spiritual leaders work from God's agenda (Heb. 11:24-26). Note: Other Scriptures may also highlight these elements of Moses' leadership.☊

4. State that Jesus is our primary model for leadership (Day Four). Point out the key to Jesus' leadership was the relationship He had with God the Father. State that Jesus allowed neither others' opinions nor Satan

to distract Him from His God-given mission. Using the material on page 28, lead a discussion of how Satan tried to distract Jesus from His mission. Ask: *How does Satan similarly try to sidetrack us from carrying out God's will today?*

5. Point out that prayer was the cornerstone of Jesus' relationship with God. Call on volunteers to read Matthew 14:23; 26:36,39; Luke 6:12; Mark 1:35; and John 17:1. Discuss the importance of prayer to our relationship with God and lead the class to brainstorm steps to strengthen their prayer lives.◉

6. Emphasize that our prayers should focus on accomplishing God's agenda, not our own, as Jesus taught in the Lord's Prayer and in His radical obedience to God. Call on volunteers to read Matthew 6:10; 26:39. State that those who put that prayer into action would be like the first-century Christians who radically obeyed God and turned their world upside down.◑ Read the quote in the margin of page 31.

7. Ask participants to reflect on the bolded question on page 31 (Are you following God's agenda or your own?). In a short period of silent reflection and prayer, give participants time to consider what is holding them back from a total surrender to God's agenda and then to respond to God in radical obedience.

8. Ask learners to review the Concepts for Consideration on page 31. Ask: *Do any of these concepts challenge your current views of leadership? Will any of them change the way you approach your God-given responsibilities as a leader? Explain.*

9. Close in prayer. Ask God to reveal unique leadership opportunities to those in the class and to embolden participants to accept those opportunities for Him.

After the Session

If you know a learner who may be struggling with a direction in which God may be leading him or her, pray for that person specifically. As appropriate, contact that person to encourage him or her.

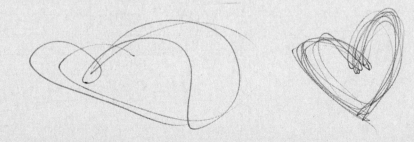

The Leader's Preparation: How God Develops Leaders

DAY ONE

The Making of a Leader: Innate Qualities

Certainly leadership involves some specific skills, but ultimately leadership is more about "being" than about "doing."

The greatness of an organization will be directly proportional to the greatness of its leader. It is rare for organizations to rise above their leaders. Giant organizations do not emerge under pygmy leaders; therefore, the key to growing an organization is to grow its leaders. Certainly leadership involves some specific skills, but ultimately leadership is more about "being" than about "doing."

The question is: how do people become leaders? Are certain people endowed with natural leadership ability? Are some people born to lead, or is leadership a set of skills that anyone can learn?

Do you see yourself as a leader? Why or why not? _Not really I'm too shy, but I am strong will..._

There is little doubt that some people display an early aptitude for leadership. Many world leaders demonstrated precipitant signs of leadership ability. When Winston Churchill was a child, he staged elaborate battlefield maneuvers with fifteen hundred toy soldiers and became engrossed in politics at an unusually young age.

LOLS H

An examination of the early lives of famous leaders usually reveals telltale signs that they were oriented to be leaders. Indeed, the next generation of great leaders is already evolving, but today's adults may be too preoccupied to notice. If churches are concerned about future leaders, they would do well to nurture their children, for any strategy for developing spiritual leaders must take into account those emerging leaders currently in their preteens.

Jacob's son, Joseph, was obviously destined to be a leader. God gave him dreams indicating he would one day be a great man. More specifically, his dreams revealed that he would lead his ten older brothers (Gen. 37:5-11).

Even though Joseph's vision for a great future was not enthusiastically shared by his older siblings, years later they would stand trembling before Joseph, the highest ranking official in Egypt, depending on him for their very survival. Then they probably wished they had taken Joseph's leadership potential more seriously while he was a youth.

Contemporary leadership writing reveals that most scholars believe leaders are both born *and* made. Although certain factors outside their control come to bear on people, predisposing them to lead, there are other factors, within people's control that, if developed, can significantly enhance their leadership ability. The media often portray leaders to the public as unusually gifted, charismatic, physically imposing and attractive people. This skewed image of leadership can lead to self-doubt on the part of many would-be leaders. Reality, however, suggests that most people can exercise leadership in some arena of life if they are willing to grow as people and to develop certain leadership skills.

> Most people can exercise leadership in some arena of life if they are willing to grow as people and to develop certain leadership skills.

What innate qualities do you possess that enhance your leadership ability? I don't get this question..

What traits do you have that may limit your leadership ability?
SHYNESS! SHYNESS ALL THE WAY!

DAY TWO

The Making of a Leader: Life Experiences

Home Life. The influence of a leader's childhood home cannot be underrated as a major factor in leadership development. While some great leaders grew up in wholesome, supportive environments, many did not.

A significant number of well-known Christian leaders grew up in dysfunctional homes. Many of these leaders have experienced God's healing grace, which has transformed them into healthy, successful leaders. Others, for whatever reason, are unwilling or feel unable to allow God's grace to free them from their troublesome pasts. These people emerge as adults with feelings of inferiority, inadequacy, and anger, all despite their outward success.

Failures. Failure is a powerful force in the making of a leader. The failure itself is not the issue; it's what failure leads to that is so determinative in leadership development. For true leaders, failure will not destroy them but will, instead, further develop their character. Abraham Lincoln's failures are well documented. In his first attempt at elected office, Lincoln placed eighth in a field of thirteen candidates. When he ran for president, 10 states did not even carry his name on the ballot. Bob Jones, president of Bob Jones University, pronounced the young Billy Graham a failure to his face, telling him he would never amount to anything.

Identify a past failure in your life and how it has affected your leadership ablility for good or for bad. _____

_____

_____

_____

_____

_____

_____

Crises. Events beyond a person's control can have the same effect as failures. They can either crush an aspiring leader or they can develop the character and resolve within the emerging leader that enables him to reach greater heights in the future. Franklin Roosevelt, considered by some to be one of America's most successful twentieth-century presidents, suffered from debilitating polio that left him in a wheelchair.

Personal Struggles. Surprisingly, perhaps, many of history's famous leaders experienced difficulty in public speaking as children. Winston Churchill, famous for his eloquence, had a speech impediment as a boy. D. L. Moody showed no early signs of developing into the forceful speaker he would become later in life. When the young Moody attempted to speak in public during his church's prayer meeting, he noted that it made adults "squirm their shoulders when I got up." Some of the adults complained that Moody did not know enough grammar to address the congregation, and he was eventually asked to abstain from commenting in public.[1]

What do you think is your greatest liability in becoming a spiritual leader? _____

_____

How do you think God might want to use this difficulty to make you more dependent on Him? _____

_____

_____

_____

_____

Success Through Hardship. Moses, arguably the greatest figure in the Old Testament, had a life filled with adversity and failure. As a newborn, his life was threatened, so his mother gave him away to a foreigner. His bungled attempt to rescue a fellow Hebrew meant he had to flee for his life into the desert. Moses spent 40 years herding sheep in the wilderness for his father-in-law because of a mistake he made in his youth. He spent another 40 years wandering in the wilderness because of a mistake made by those he was leading. He would ultimately die outside the land he had dreamed of entering because of a mistake he made while wandering in the wilderness. Yet, despite his significant failures, even secular historians recognize Moses as one of the most influential leaders of all time.

It would be a mistake to conclude that hardship and failure always produce successful leaders, just as it would be simplistic to assume that good leaders emerge only out of adversity. The key to leadership development lies not in the experiences, but in peoples' responses to those experiences. Failure and personal crises do not disqualify people from becoming leaders. Rather, God can use adversity to build certain qualities deep within one's character that could not be fully developed in any other way.

Describe how you have grown through adversity you have experienced._____

_____

_____

_____

_____

DAY THREE

God's Work in Leaders' Lives

God Gives His Holy Spirit. Although life experiences impact general leadership abilities, there is an added dimension to the growth of a spiritual leader. That dimension is the active work of the Holy Spirit in leaders' lives. Oswald Sanders notes: "There is no such thing as a self-made spiritual leader."[2]

"There is no such thing as a self-made spiritual leader." –Oswald Sanders

Read the quote in the margin. Although there may be self-made worldly leaders, why is it true that there is no such thing as a self-made spiritual leader? _____

_____

_____

_____

_____

Spiritual ends require spiritual means, and spiritual means come only by the Holy Spirit. This truth is evident in God's message to Zerubbabel, the governor over Jerusalem, who oversaw the rebuilding of the temple after the Jewish exiles' return from Babylon. Zerubbabel was confronted with the doubly daunting task of governing a region decimated by war and exile, as well as rebuilding a massive temple that lay in ruins. At this critical juncture, he received this message from God: "'Not by might nor by power, but by My Spirit,' says the Lord of hosts." (Zech. 4:6). Zerubbabel learned an invaluable lesson—spiritual leaders require the Spirit to work in their lives even when they are performing what appear to be unspiritual tasks. Without the Spirit's presence, people may be leaders, but they are not spiritual leaders.

> Spiritual ends require spiritual means, and spiritual means come only by the Holy Spirit.

What evidence is there in your life that you are leading in the power of the Holy Spirit and not out of your own strength?

_____

_____

_____

_____

_____

God Sets the Leader's Agenda. When God directs a life for His purposes, all of life is a school. No experience, good or bad, is ever wasted (Rom. 8:28). God doesn't squander people's time. He doesn't ignore their pain. He brings not only healing but growth out of even the worst experiences. Every relationship can be God's instrument to mature a person's character. The world can offer its best theories on leadership and provide the most extensive training possible, but unless God sets the agenda for a leader's life, that person, though thoroughly educated, will not be an effective spiritual leader.

God Gives the Assignment. People may become leaders by responding in a healthy manner to all they encounter in life, but they will not become spiritual leaders unless God calls them to this role and equips them for it. Secular leadership is something to which people can aspire. It can be achieved through sheer force of will. Spiritual leadership, on the other hand, is not a role for which one applies. Rather, it is assigned by God.

Historically, God has chosen ordinary people, most of whom were not looking for a divine assignment. Nevertheless, God saw something in their hearts that led Him to assign particular tasks. While there is nothing wrong with wanting to experience God working powerfully in one's life, those wishing for God to use them mightily should not pursue leadership positions in God's kingdom. They should seek God with all their hearts and wait upon His will. The greatest area of concern for spiritual leaders is their hearts. When God sees people with righteous lives, He may exercise His prerogative to show Himself strong in their lives in order to accomplish His divine will.

DAY FOUR

The Example of Abraham

Abraham's life provides a thorough example of how God chooses ordinary people and turns them into effective spiritual leaders.

Abraham Was an Ordinary Person. Abraham was born in Ur, among the moon-worshiping Chaldeans. Abraham's agenda for his life was probably not complicated. He likely planned to live out his days raising his herds and flocks. God's agenda was radically different from Abraham's. To say that God's plans dwarfed Abraham's plans would be an understatement! The key was not for God to bless Abraham's plans but for Abraham to discard his agenda in favor of God's will.

Abraham Built on His Heritage. When God first spoke to Abraham and told him to leave his homeland in Ur, God had already used Abraham's father, Terah, to begin the process (Gen. 11:31-32; Acts 7:2-4). What God began with Abraham's father, He continued through Abraham's life and eventually completed through Abraham's descendants. Heritage can be a powerful factor in leadership. As in Abraham's case, God may begin a work in one generation that is brought to fruition in succeeding generations. God wanted Abraham to go to Canaan, so He also gave that desire to Abraham's father. God called a son to be a nomad, so He initiated a restlessness in the father.

Abraham Grew Through Failure. Every event in Abraham's life contributed to his character development. Abraham did not begin his life as a paragon of faith, but gradually, over many years, he developed a mature and deep relationship with God. God used Abraham's failures to prepare him for leadership. For example, God specifically instructed Abraham to leave his family behind but instead Abraham took Lot with him to Canaan (Gen. 12:1,4). With this one act of seemingly minor disobedience, Abraham inadvertently endangered the inheritance God wanted to give him and his descendants. Abraham learned a valuable lesson regarding his modification of God's will. Adding to God's will is as devastating as rejecting God's will.

Abraham Learned by Experience. Abraham's understanding of God was not theoretical. He didn't learn it from books. He learned it through encounters with God. Each time God revealed a new facet of His character to Abraham; it was through experience. For example, God gave Abraham a brilliant victory over a superior army. Thereafter, Abraham knew he could trust God as his shield (Gen. 15:1). Spiritual leaders must make the connection between God's activity in their lives and God's character.

Abraham Was Not Allowed to Take Shortcuts. Genesis 16 details a low point in Abraham's life. Despite the covenant God made with him to make him the father of countless descendents, the fact was that he remained childless. Abraham listened to the counsel of people instead of listening to God. His wife, Sarah, advised him to produce a child through her servant Hagar. It was worldly reasoning at its best, but it was not God's way. Abraham chose to take a shortcut rather than to trust God's word.

Abraham was 100 years old when Isaac was born. He had waited 25 years for God to carry out His promise. Abraham learned a lesson about the difference between God's timing and people's timing.

Describe a time when you learned a lesson about the difference between God's timing and your timing. _____

_____

_____

_____ .

God sees things from an eternal perspective. People see things from a temporal view. Spiritual leaders court disaster when they panic and assume they must take matters in their own hands. When spiritual leaders wait patiently on the Lord, regardless of how long it takes, God always proves Himself absolutely true to His word. Many more leaders would see major accomplishments occur in their lives and in their organizations if only they were willing to wait as long as necessary to see God accomplish His will.

Abraham Obeyed God. Through obedience, people experience God working through their lives and they come to know more about God's character. In response to Abraham's obedience, God spared Isaac's life (Gen. 22). Far more hinged on Abraham's obedience than he first realized. Abraham came to understand that his actions did not affect him alone, but his obedience to God would impact generations to follow.

Abraham Became a Friend of God. It is one thing to call God your friend. It is quite another for God to call you his friend. Abraham is the only person to whom Scripture gives this distinction (Jas. 2:23).

God didn't choose Abraham because of his leadership ability. He chose Abraham because of his heart. The key was not that Abraham attended all the best leadership seminars. The key was that he came to know God and he allowed God to transform him into a leader through his obedience. When people strive to have their hearts right before God, then God promises to "show Himself strong" (2 Chron. 16:9, hcsb).

> God didn't choose Abraham because of his leadership ability. He chose Abraham because of his heart.

DAY FIVE

Conclusion

God appoints leaders. People may apply for various leadership positions, but God is the One who ultimately determines which leadership roles they will have. Leadership development comes through character development, because leadership is a character issue. Therefore, the first truth in leadership development is this: God's assignments are always based on character—the greater the character, the greater the assignment (Luke 16:10). Before God will give leaders larger assignments, He will build in them greater characters. No role is more important than that of a spiritual leader; therefore, God will first build a character that is capable of handling such a meaningful assignment.

> Leadership development comes through character development, because leadership is a character issue.

Character building can be a slow, sometimes painful process. But the person willing to allow God to complete the process will know the joy of being used by God. Even better, those who submit their lives to God's refining process will experience the profound joy that comes with knowing God in a deeply personal way.

Character building takes time. There are no shortcuts. Two factors determine the length of time required for God to develop character worthy of spiritual leadership—trust in God and obedience to God.

God builds character through the ordinary experiences and crises of life. Most character building does not occur while one is attending a seminar or taking a course. Rather, God uses everyday events, both good and bad, to shape leaders. Often these events are situations that are beyond peoples' control—events that require people to place their trust in God.

God does not always intervene when people are determined to go in a harmful direction, but He is always available to redeem people. Through the redemption process, they learn more about themselves and more about God. Wise leaders allow God to make the most of their mistakes. Those willing to submit themselves to the leadership development track of the Lord have the potential of growing into the leaders God wants them to become.

> Two factors determine the length of time required for God to develop character worthy of spiritual leadership—trust in God and obedience to God.

Write a brief prayer in the margin expressing your desire to grow into the leader God wants you to be and your willingness to submit to His plan of leadership development.

Concepts for Consideration

- Ultimately, leadership is more about "being" than about "doing."
- Any strategy for developing spiritual leaders must take into account those emerging leaders currently in their preteens.
- Most of history's famous leaders have been decidedly ordinary people.
- God can use adversity to build certain qualities deep within one's character that could not be fully developed in any other way.
- No experience, good or bad, is ever wasted.
- People may apply for various leadership positions, but God is the One who ultimately determines which leadership roles they will have.
- God's assignments are always based on character—the greater the character, the greater the assignment.

1. John Pollock, *Moody* (Grand Rapids: Baker Books, 1963), 31.
2. J. Oswald Sanders, *Spiritual Leadership* (Chicago: Moody, 1967), 33.

LEADER GUIDE

Before the Session

1. Write the following statement on a sentence strip: "There is no such thing as a self-made spiritual leader" (Oswald Sanders).

2. Write the following statements on a poster board or white board:

   "Abraham was an ordinary person" (Gen. 11:27-30).

   "Abraham built on his heritage" (Gen. 11:31-32).

   "Abraham grew through failure" (Gen. 12:1,4).

   "Abraham learned by experience" (Gen. 14:14-16; 15:1).

   "Abraham was not allowed to take shortcuts" (Gen. 16:1-3).

   "Abraham obeyed God" (Gen. 22:1-2,9-12).

   "Abraham became a friend of God"(James 2:23).

During the Session

1. State that this is the third week in a six-week study of leadership. As time allows, give an overview of the previous two weeks (The Leader's Challenge and The Leader's Role). Point to the poster with the title of this week's lesson: "The Leader's Preparation." Ask the question: *Are leaders born or made?* After brief discussion, state that according to Blackaby, leaders are both born and made. Call on a volunteer to read Genesis 37:5-11. State that God clearly had plans for Joseph to become a leader, but those plans took years to unfold. Call on another volunteer to read Psalm 139:13-16. Ask: *How can we use the truths of these two Scriptures to encourage not only ourselves but also others to be sensitive to opportunities for leadership that God places in our lives?*

2. Tell participants to get into small groups of three or four. Assign each group one of the five life experiences described by Blackaby on pages 36-37 (home life, failures, crises, personal struggles, hardship). Then ask the groups to share personal examples of how those experiences helped shape their lives. Next, direct each group to discuss one leader in the Bible who was shaped by any of these five life experiences. Characters to consider include Moses (Ex. 2), David (2 Sam. 11), Esther (Esth. 2), Paul (Acts 8:1-3; 22:2-5), or Peter (John 18:15-18). After a few minutes,

call on groups to tell the class about the biblical leader discussed. Call on volunteers to read Jeremiah 29:11 and Romans 8:28 and briefly discuss how those words encourage Christians facing personal struggles and hardship.◯

3. State that although life experiences impact general leadership abilities, there is an added dimension to the growth of a spiritual leader—the Holy Spirit in leaders' lives. Draw attention to the sentence strip with the statement by Oswald Sanders. Ask participants to respond to the bolded question at the bottom of page 38.

4. Call on a volunteer to read Zechariah 4:6. Briefly describe the historical context of this Scripture (For help, go to *mystudybible.com.*) Share with the class about a time when you relied on the Holy Spirit for a particular task for which you knew you were unqualified. Invite participants to share similar experiences.

5. State that Abraham's life provides a good example of how God chooses ordinary people and turns them into effective spiritual leaders. Call on a volunteer to read Hebrews 11:8-12,17-19 and James 2:21-23 for a short summary of Abraham's life. Draw attention to the poster with the statements about Abraham. As you read each statement aloud, ask a volunteer to read aloud the appropriate Scripture. Add explanatory comments from the material in Day Four (pp. 40-42). Proceed through each of the seven statements. Invite learners to share a life lesson that God is teaching them based on Abraham's life.◯

6. Review the Concepts for Consideration on page 43. Ask learners to share which of the statements gives them the greatest encouragement and which one presents the greatest challenge.

7. Using the material in Day Five, emphasize that leadership development comes through character development. Call attention to the quote in the margin of page 43. Close in prayer, asking God to develop the class members into the leaders He wants them to be.

After the Session

Pray about an individual you may mentor to become a Christian leader. As God reveals that person to you, take steps to begin that mentoring relationship.

The Leader's Vision: Where Do Leaders Get It and How Do They Communicate It?

DAY ONE

Where Do Leaders Obtain Their Vision?

When it comes to vision, no statement is more frequently quoted (or misquoted) by Christians and non-Christians alike than King Solomon's observation: "Where there is no vision, the people perish" (Prov. 29:18, kjv). Scripture's timeless wisdom once again proves relevant to modern life. Leadership pundits claim vision is crucial for an obvious reason: if you can't see where you are going, you are unlikely to get there. Vision can serve as the North Star for organizations, helping leaders keep their bearings as they move their people forward. Hence, any organization that does not have a clear vision of where it is going is in danger of becoming sidetracked and failing to accomplish its purpose.

Vision is critical for organizations, so it stands to reason that leaders must be visionaries. But where do leaders find visions that inspire people and unite them to great accomplishments? There are many sources from which leaders draw their vision.

Duplicating Success. Some leaders borrow their visions. They do things the way they do because that's the way they've always done it. The

> If you can't see where you are going, you are unlikely to get there.

easiest course of action is often the one taken previously, especially if it was successful. But sometimes success becomes the leader's greatest enemy.

Churches are remiss if they assume that because God worked mightily in a particular way in the past, He will choose to work in exactly the same way in the present. Many organizations today are locked into doing things a certain way, not because it is still effective, but because it was effective yesterday.

> Many organizations today are locked into doing things a certain way, not because it is still effective, but because it was effective yesterday.

Can you name one example of how your church is locked into doing something in a certain way, not because it is still effective, but because it was effective in the past? _____

_____

_____

_____

Vanity. Some leaders set the goals for their organization based on what will bring them the most personal success or praise. Countless businesses have crumbled under leaders who were motivated by vanity rather than by vision. Churches have been saddled with crippling debts as they sought to repay bills incurred by former pastors looking to make a name for themselves.

Need. Businesses find out what people are seeking, then they develop a product to meet the expressed need. While this has long been a profitable practice for secular businesses, Christian organizations are increasingly favoring the need-based approach in determining their vision. Churches survey their communities to discover the needs of the people, then compile, categorize, and prioritize the data. Then they set the church's agenda in response to the survey's results.

Using the expressed needs of a target audience to establish an organization's vision is not a foolproof approach, however. While churches must be sensitive to the needs in their communities, a need expressed is not the same thing as a call by God.

Available Resources. The availability of resources sometimes induces vision. That is, organizations gravitate toward certain activities or priorities simply because resources such as manpower, or finances, or equipment are available to them. Church programs are often motivated in this manner. As a general rule, resources should follow vision, not determine it. Leaders must first decide the vision for their organization and then marshal the necessary resources to achieve it. Foolish leaders will thought-lessly accept resources and then try to piece together a vision that uses the resources they have accumulated.

Is your church's vision currently being determined by available resources? In what ways? _____

_____

_____

_____

_____

Leader-Driven. Many people assume that being a visionary leader involves personally developing a vision for one's organization. But leaders' best thinking will not build the kingdom of God. Why? Because people do not naturally think the way God does. The apostle Paul observed, "Where is the wise man? Where is the scribe? Where is the debater of this age? Has not God made foolish the wisdom of the world?" (1 Cor. 1:20). God's ways are completely different from man's ways. When people "think great thoughts *for* God" and "dream great dreams *for* God," the emphasis is on dreams and goals that originate from people rather than from God. Every time leaders choose to develop their own vision for their people instead of seeking God's will, they are giving their people their best thinking instead of God's. That is a poor exchange indeed.

DAY TWO

God's Revelation

God does not ask His followers to operate by vision. *God's people live by revelation.*

The previous sources of vision have one thing in common—they are all generated by worldly thinking. This is not surprising; *the world functions by vision.* But God does not ask His followers to operate by vision. *God's people live by revelation.* Proverbs 29:18, although widely used, is also widely misapplied. The popular translation is, "Where there is no vision, the people perish" (KJV). A more accurate translation of the Hebrew is: "Where there is no revelation, the people cast off restraint" (NIV). There is a significant difference between revelation and vision. Vision is something people produce; revelation is something people receive. Leaders can dream up a vision, but they cannot discover God's will. God must reveal it. Throughout the remainder of this book, the term *vision* will continue to be used, but it will not connote the popular idea of a leader-generated goal or dream. Instead, vision will be used to refer to what God has revealed and promised about the future. The visions that drive spiritual leaders must be derived from God.

Describe in your own words the difference between vision and revelation. _____

_____

_____

_____

Many Christian leaders adopt the world's approach to vision and miss out on God's way. In seeking to serve God, they inadvertently try to take on the responsibility of God. The truth is, God is on mission to redeem humanity. He is the only One who knows how to do it. Leaders must understand, as Christ did, that their role is to seek the Father's will and to adjust their lives to Him. Being proactive by nature, leaders want to rush into action. As a result, they don't spend enough time seeking to hear clearly from God. Instead, they simply have a cursory moment of prayer and then begin making their plans. They seek out a few relevant Scriptures and hurry into the goal-setting phase, falsely confident that because they incorporated prayer and Scripture into their goal-setting process, their plans are "of God."

Asking God to set one's goals and to bless one's dreams does not ensure that they are from God. Only God can reveal His plans and He does so in His way, on His time schedule, and to whom He wills. How often do Christian leaders claim to have received their vision from God when in fact they have simply dreamed up the most desirable future they could imagine and then prayed for God to bless their efforts as they set out to achieve it? It is critical for leaders to walk closely with the Father, so they are keenly aware of His revelation and are ready to respond in obedience

SCRIPTURE

"Without revelation people run wild" (Prov. 29:18, HCSB).

"When people do not accept divine guidance, they run wild" (Prov. 29:18, NLT).

How often do Christian leaders claim to have received their vision from God when in fact they have simply dreamed up the most desirable future they could imagine and then prayed for God to bless their efforts as they set out to achieve it?

to His initiatives. The role of spiritual leaders is not to dream up dreams for God but to be the vanguard for their people in understanding God's revelation. The leader's job is to communicate God's promise to the people, not to create the vision and then strive to enlist people to buy in to it.

What is your church's God-given vision?_____

_____

_____

_____

What is God calling your class to do to help accomplish that vision? _____

_____

_____

_____

What is God calling you to do personally to help accomplish that vision? _____

_____

_____

_____

DAY THREE

How Does Vision Inspire and Move People?

Great visions move people. John F. Kennedy's vision to place a man on the moon by the end of the decade mobilized a nation to accomplish the seemingly impossible. Martin Luther King Jr.'s "I have a dream" speech on the steps of the Lincoln Memorial before 250,000 people electrified his listeners and shook his nation.

The challenge for leaders is to understand how vision can motivate followers to do things they would never attempt otherwise. Vision statements are not enough. Such statements, generally decreed from the top down, have little effect on those who work for the organization each day. Even when the organizations' members are allowed to give input into the development of vision statements, often this is little more than an exercise wherein the administration merely guides people to a preestablished conclusion.

Many lofty vision statements carry no innate appeal to the people lower down in the organization. Companies can generate goals such as "Five percent gain in market share next year" or "10 percent less waste next year." These goals may be worthwhile, but they do not carry with them any obvious personal benefit to those being asked to do the work. Churches do the same thing: "10 percent increase in membership" or "reach the second phase of our capital campaign." As James Champy said, "Numbers by themselves never mobilize anyone but an accountant."[1] Vision must be clear, compelling, and common to all the people.

The problem with many organizations is that they ask their people to make great sacrifices on behalf of puny visions. They encourage their people to give their best but fail to spell out any clear benefit. Moreover, it can appear to those laboring in support of the vision that those benefiting the most from their efforts are the ones promoting the vision. Leaders often fail to appeal to people's innate need to believe they have made a valuable contribution to society. People want their lives to make a difference.

To the world, a good vision is an image of something that is both desirable and attainable. The difference between worldly visions and God-given visions is that God-given visions are always impossible to achieve apart from God. In this regard, Christian leaders have a tremendous advantage over secular leaders. People want to be a part of something significant. People want their lives to make a difference in their world. People want to be a part of something God is doing. If it is clear that God has made a promise to a group of people, there should be little difficulty in enlisting the support of group members.

> The difference between worldly visions and God-given visions is that God-given visions are always impossible to achieve apart from God.

Have you ever been personally involved in a God-given vision that would have been impossible to achieve apart from God? Explain.

_____

_____

_____

_____

DAY FOUR

How Do Leaders Communicate Vision?

Sometimes spiritual leaders spend a lot of energy trying to get their people to "buy in" to their vision because their vision is not from God. In the Christian context, the process of selling a vision is flawed. If a vision must be sold to others, it is not a compelling vision and is probably not from God. Spiritual leaders don't sell vision; they share what God has revealed to them and trust that the Holy Spirit will confirm that same vision in the hearts of their people. Today, Christian leaders often develop a vision for their organizations and then demand the members either get on board or find another organization. This approach could not be further from the New Testament pattern. Spiritual leaders know they cannot change people; only the Holy Spirit can do this. If the Holy Spirit is not convincing people to follow in a new direction, it may be that God is not the author of the new direction. Secular writers agree that selling vision is difficult. Peter Senge observes that "90 percent of the time, what passes for commitment is compliance."[2]

People may change their behavior in response to a leader's encouragement, but that doesn't mean they have changed their core values and beliefs. Values go deep—they will not be altered by a memo or sales pitch. People either believe something, or they don't. God's people either hear from God, or they don't. Either people have moved on to God's agenda, or they haven't.

Establishing that the leader's role is not to set the vision or to sell the vision begs the question: "What is the spiritual leader's role?" It is to bear witness to what God says. Spiritual leaders must bring followers into a face-to-face encounter with God so they hear from God directly, not indirectly through their leader. Jesus shared the Father's revelation with His disciples corporately (John 15:15). Spiritual leaders may never convince their people they have heard from God personally, but once their people

SCRIPTURE

"I do not call you slaves anymore, because a slave doesn't know what his master is doing. I have called you friends, because I have made known to you everything I have heard from My Father" (John 15:15, HCSB).

hear from God themselves, there will be no stopping them from participating in the work God is doing. That is because the Holy Spirit will take the truth, as shared by the leader, and confirm it in the hearts of the people. The leader cannot convince people that a particular direction is from God. This is the Holy Spirit's task.

As people grow in their relationship with God, they will hear from God themselves and want to follow Him.

The key to spiritual leadership is to encourage followers to grow in their relationship with their Lord. This cannot be done by talking about God. It cannot be accomplished by exhorting people to love God. It can only be achieved when leaders bring their people face to face with God and God convinces them that He is the God of love who can be trusted.

> The key to spiritual leadership is to encourage followers to grow in their relationship with their Lord.

How are you helping others grow in their relationship with God?_____

_____

_____

DAY FIVE

Leadership Is Communication

One of the most effective ways for leaders to relate what God is doing is through the telling of stories. Often when leaders see God at work around their organization, they neglect to relate what has happened to their people. This robs the people of an exciting opportunity to experience the powerful activity of God. It also prevents them from making the connection between what God is doing and their own involvement in the organization. The power of stories is that they appeal both to the mind and the heart.

Wise leaders continually help their people see how God is working in their midst. Leaders can do this by telling stories—true stories of how God has worked in the past and how God is working at present. Leaders also link what God has done and is doing with what He has promised to do in the future. The Book of Deuteronomy is essentially a series of sermons in which Moses recounted to the Israelites all God had done for them up to that point. Joshua, Moses' successor, continued the tradition. In Joshua 24:1-13, the old warrior recounted the entire history of the Israelites in a story in which God was the central character. After hearing all that God had done, the people were motivated to move forward to see what God would do next!

Read Joshua 24:1-13 and summarize what Joshua told the Israelites. Why does recounting such history lessons motivate people to move forward with God?_____

_____

_____

_____

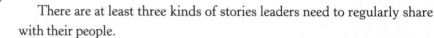

SCRIPTURE

"All that He does is splendid and majestic; His righteousness endures forever. He has caused His wonderful works to be remembered. The LORD is gracious and compassionate" (Ps. 111:3-4, HCSB).

There are at least three kinds of stories leaders need to regularly share with their people.

1. *Stories from the past.* Leaders should relate stories from the past as Moses and Joshua did. What has God done for that organization throughout its history? (See Ps. 111:3-4).

How has God worked in your church in the past?_____

_____

_____

_____

2. *Stories for the present.* Leaders should also share stories relating to the present. What is God doing right now? Leaders should never assume their people will automatically make the connection between what is happening in their midst and God's activity. The leader's role is to help people make the connection.

How is God active in your church right now? _____

_____

_____

_____

3. *Stories that light the future.* Third, leaders should hold before the people images of the future. When spiritual leaders relate stories of the future, they are not simply describing a desirable future. Rather, they are relating what God has indicated He intends to do. For spiritual leaders, all past, present, and future stories should come from God and be God-centered.

What do you sense God is wanting to do in your church in the future? What will it look like when He accomplishes His purposes?_____

_____

_____

_____

Vision is crucial for an organization. Its source is God's revelation of His activity. God's revelation can usually be stated as a promise and can be expressed through an image. When leaders successfully communicate vision to their people, it will be God who sets the agenda for the organization, not the leader, and the people will know it is God.

Concepts for Consideration
- The world functions by vision; God's people live by revelation.
- Vision is something people produce; revelation is something people receive.
- Leaders can dream up a vision, but they cannot discover God's will. God must reveal it.
- The role of spiritual leaders is not to dream up dreams for God, but to be the vanguard for their people in understanding God's revelation.
- God's promises are impossible to achieve apart from Him.
- The problem with many organizations is that they ask their people to make great sacrifices on behalf of puny visions.
- People want to be a part of something God is doing.
- Spiritual leaders cannot prove that God has spoken to them. They can only bear witness to what God said. The key to spiritual leadership is bringing people into a face-to-face encounter with God so that they hear from God directly and not indirectly through the leader.

1. James Champy, *Reengineering Management: The Mandate for New Leadership* (New York: HarperBusiness, 1995), 55.
2. Peter Senge, *The Fifth Discipline: The Art and Practice of the Learning Organization* (New York: Currency Doubleday, paperback ed., 1994), 218.

LEADER GUIDE

Before the Session

1. Gather several translations of the Bible.

2. Make a sentence strip with the following statement: "The world functions by vision; God's people live by revelation."

3. Invite the pastor to visit your class to share his God-given vision for your church.

4. Enlist a learner to study Joshua 24:1-13 and be prepared to share a summary of those verses with the class.

During the Session

1. State that this is the fourth week in a six-week study of leadership. Begin the session by saying that a blind person once asked St. Anthony: "Can there be anything worse than losing eyesight?" He replied: "Yes, losing your vision." Point to the poster with the lesson's title and say that today's lesson will focus on the leader's vision.

2. Call attention to the quote in the margin of page 46: "If you can't see where you are going, you are unlikely to get there." Vision is critical for churches. But where do church leaders find vision? Ask learners to identify the five worldly sources of vision Blackaby discussed on pages 46-48. Call for responses to the two bolded questions in Day One (pp. 47,48).

3. Point to the sentence strip and read it aloud: "The world functions by vision; God's people live by revelation." Distribute the various translations of the Bible and call on participants to read Proverbs 29:18. Write the variations of the Scripture on the board as they are being read. Challenge learners to explain the meaning of that verse in one sentence and lead in a brief discussion about the difference between vision and revelation. Emphasize that the visions that drive spiritual leaders must be derived from God. God sets the agenda for the church, not the leader. Leaders themselves do not establish the vision; their role is to communicate it and to bring followers into deeper relationship with God so they hear from God themselves (Day Four).

4. Briefly discuss how in today's rushed world, we are tempted to run ahead of God before truly hearing from Him. Call on volunteers to read the following Scripture passages: Psalm 27:14; 46:10; and 130:5-6. Ask learners to identify the common theme in each of these Scriptures. Say that God reveals His plans in His way and on His time schedule. Ask participants to list specific and practical steps for taking the time necessary to hear from God before moving into action. ☉

5. State that when your church was started, a guiding vision directed the founding church members. Today your church continues to move forward with a vision. Ask: *What is our church's guiding vision?* (If your pastor is available, ask him to visit your class to share his God-given vision for the church.)

6. Lead the class members to discuss what they can do to be a part of accomplishing the church's vision. As ideas for possible outreach opportunities, as well as ideas for possible service opportunities within the church, emerge, assign specific people to follow up on those ideas and report back to the class. Remind participants that, just as God may be calling the class to do its part in accomplishing the God-given vision for the church, He also calls each Christian individually to do his or her part. Challenge participants to prayerfully consider what God may be calling them to do personally in regard to the church's vision. ◐ ●

7. Say that wise leaders continually help people see how God is working in their midst. Joshua did this in Joshua 24. Call on the person enlisted ahead of time to summarize what Joshua told the Israelites in Joshua 24:1-13. Write the words "past," "present" and "future" on the board. Discuss: *How has God worked in our church in the past? How is God actively working in our church right now? What do you sense God is wanting to do in our church in the future?*

8. Review the Concepts for Consideration on page 55. Ask learners to tell which of the concepts presents the greatest challenge for your church at the present moment.

9. Close in prayer, asking God to reveal His vision to leaders in your church and learners in your class.

The Leader's Character: A Life That Moves Others to Follow

DAY ONE

Illegitimate Sources of Influence

"I have met many of the great men of my time, but Lee alone impressed me with the feeling that I was in the presence of a man who was cast in a grander mold, and made of different and finer metal than all other men."[1] This was the observation of Field Marshall Viscount Wolseley after he met Robert E. Lee. Lee's leadership is fascinating because even though he was grossly underequipped in both manpower and supplies, he rarely lost a battle. Even more impressive is that, though they were overwhelmingly outnumbered and though they received few benefits, his soldiers were fiercely loyal to him throughout the Civil War. Even when the war was lost and it was futile to resist the vastly larger and better-equipped Union army, Lee's soldiers were prepared to continue fighting if he would only give the orders.

What inspired such loyalty among Lee's followers? One thing is certain: it was not his rank as general. Other generals did not enjoy such loyalty from their troops. Nor was it Lee's ability to court-martial traitors; he was generally loath to do it. It is best concluded the key was Lee *himself*. Lee's soldiers followed him because of who he was.

The catchword for leadership today is *influence*. But how do people achieve influence over others?

What does it mean to be a person of influence? _____

_____

Whom in your life do you regularly have opportunity to influence? _____

Personal influence can come from several sources, some legitimate, others questionable. Three illegitimate sources of influence are position, power, and personality.

> Three illegitimate sources of influence are position, power, and personality.

Previous generations generally associated authority and influence with position. Bosses were automatically respected by virtue of their position. In spiritual matters, people trusted their ministers implicitly and offered them reverence as a matter of course. The sad truth is that many Christian organizations and churches are led by people who sought an office for all the wrong reasons. If there are any leaders who should not rely upon their position for their influence, it is spiritual leaders. Spiritual leadership is based on the work of the Holy Spirit and on spiritual character. Without the guiding, empowering presence of the Spirit, leaders may hold positions but they will not be spiritual leaders.

Some leaders pursue influence by using force and manipulation. Spiritual dictatorships can be the most oppresive form of tyranny. Some Christian leaders believe God delegates His authority to leaders, obligating followers to submit unquestioningly as if they were obeying God Himself. Although God chooses to work through leaders to accomplish His purposes, obeying a leader is not necessarily equal to obeying God. There is no substitute for a personal relationship with God as He exercises His lordship directly over His followers.

People often follow leaders strictly because of their charisma and winsome personalities. The popularity of a leader is not in itself a bad thing, but it cannot be the only thing. Leaders must offer more to their people than charm. By itself, an engaging personality is not enough to constitute spiritual leadership.

When organizations are built around the personality of a leader, not only is the organization susceptible to the weaknesses and whims of its leader, but it also faces an inevitable crisis when the leader leaves the organization.

This important principle is relevant for churches seeking new pastors. Christ said He would build His church (Matt. 16:18). In order to thrive, churches do not need leaders who exude charm. In fact, choosing a pastor based solely on personality is choosing to build a church on a person rather than on Christ.

Position, power, and personality are all misconceived sources of influence for leaders. What then are the standards by which true spiritual leaders can be measured? Christian leaders should demonstrate specific characteristics that confirm their legitimacy as spiritual leaders.

What problems might come to leaders who rely only on position, power, or personality to influence others? _____

_____

_____

_____

DAY TWO

A Legitimate Source of Influence: God's Authentication

The first and most important test of legitimacy for spiritual leaders is God's authentication. There are numerous biblical and secular examples of men and women whom God affirmed as genuine spiritual leaders.

> Moses' accomplishments as a spiritual leader came from the depth of his relationship with God, not from the strength of his personality.

Moses could not attribute his success to his own leadership abilities, for he was not naturally gifted as a leader. By his own admission, he was a poor public speaker (Ex. 4:10); he was inept at delegating (Ex. 18:13-27); he had a temper problem (Ex. 32:19; Num. 20:9-13). Worst of all, he was a murderer. Nevertheless, Moses' accomplishments as a spiritual leader came from the depth of his relationship with God, not from the strength of his personality. Scripture indicates that "the Lord used to speak to Moses face to face, just as a man speaks to his friend" (Ex. 33:11). The Israelites recognized Moses' close walk with God. Whenever Moses

would descend from the mountain after meeting with God, his face would glow with the glory of God (Ex. 34:29-35). God's presence in Moses' life was unmistakable!

What evidences of God's presence in your life are unmistakable?

_____

_____

It is imperative for spiritual leaders to evaluate their lives to determine whether God is confirming their leadership. There should be ample evidence of God's affirmation. For one thing, God will fulfill His promises to the leader and the leader's organization. Leaders who continually present new ideas and visions for the future but who never see those dreams come to fruition are clearly presenting their own visions and not God's.

Second, when God affirms a leader, God will vindicate that person's reputation over time. All leaders suffer criticism during the course of their work. Criticism is not necessarily a sign of poor leadership. It may stem from people resisting God rather than rejecting the leader. The way to tell the difference is that God will ultimately exculpate those who are led by the Spirit.

A third sign of God's presence in a leader is changed lives. When someone leads in the Spirit's power, lives are changed. Leaders may entertain people, or impress people, or even motivate people, but if there is no spiritual advancement in the people they lead, their leadership originates from the leader's talent, but not necessarily from God.

A fourth characteristic of God-inspired leadership is that others recognize God as the driving force behind the leader's agenda. When God chooses a leader who is willing to submit to His will and to trust Him to do what He promises, God is pleased to work powerfully through that leader. Leaders who are led by God will be willing to lead their people to accept God-sized assignments. Leaders who walk by sight, however, will never see God perform miracles as leaders will who walk by faith.

Finally, the unmistakable mark of leaders who are authenticated by God is that they are like Christ. They function in a Christlike manner, and those who follow them become more like Christ. The success of a spiritual leader is not measured in dollars, percentages, numbers, or attendance. A person is truly a spiritual leader when others are moved to be more like Christ.

A person is truly a spiritual leader when others are moved to be more like Christ.

How does one attain God's authentication? The key lies not in the leader, but in God. There is nothing a leader can do that will guarantee God's affirmation. All a leader can do is submit. Some spiritual leaders try to be more committed. What they need is to be more submitted. There is a significant difference between a personal determination to try harder and a complete abandonment of one's self to God's purposes. The former rests on people and their commitment; the latter relies on God and His sufficiency.

Explain in your own words the difference in *commitment* to God and *surrender* to God. _____

_____

_____

_____

Which word best describes your life? _____

❖

DAY THREE

A Legitimate Source of Influence: Encounters with God

You cannot be a spiritual leader if you are not meeting God in profound, life-changing ways.

People do not choose to become spiritual leaders. Spiritual leadership flows out of a person's vibrant, intimate relationship with God. You cannot be a spiritual leader if you are not meeting God in profound, life-changing ways.

Dwight L. Moody was experiencing great success as the director of the YMCA in Chicago. Moreover, he was pastor of a thriving church. By all appearances Moody was a successful minister of the gospel. Then in June 1871, Mrs. Sarah Anne Cooke and Mrs. Hawxhurst sat in the front row of the church and diligently prayed during the service. Moody approached them to ask the reason for such fervent prayer. They told him they were praying for him because they sensed he needed the power of the Spirit in his life and ministry. A change began to take place in Moody. He confessed, "There came a great hunger into my soul. I did not know what it was. I began to cry out as I never did before. I really felt that I did not want to live if I could not have this power for service." Moody asked the two women to pray with him every Friday afternoon until he had received the powerful anointing of the Holy Spirit.

Moody finally yielded every part of his life and will to his Lord. Suddenly, he felt the overwhelming presence of God in an unprecedented manner. Moody quickly found a room in which he could be alone with God. "The room seemed ablaze with God. He dropped to the floor and lay bathing in the Divine. Of this communion, this mount of transfiguration," Moody said, "'I can say that God revealed Himself to me, and I had such an experience of His love that I had to ask Him to stay his hand.'"[2]

It was only a few months later, while in England, that Moody heard Henry Varley's challenging words: "Moody, the world has yet to see what God will do with a man fully consecrated to him." Moody was prepared to be that man, and God used him to become the greatest evangelist of the late-nineteenth century.

God continues to look for those who are radically yielded to Him in every part of life so He may reveal His power to a watching world.

> God continues to look for those who are radically yielded to Him in every part of life so He may reveal His power to a watching world.

Review Paul's account of his conversion experience in Acts 26:13-23. Recall a personal encounter you had with God. Describe in the margin how that encounter was a part of God's transformative work in your life.

DAY FOUR

A Legitimate Source of Influence: Character/Integrity

In previous generations, the public was not generally aware of their leader's personal life, and so a leader's personal failures were not usually considered when evaluating his or her job performance. A drinking problem at home was considered a personal matter as long as the employee kept sober on the job. Prominent politicians could live immorally, yet their deceit was not widely known and not considered to significantly detract from their leadership ability. Today most leadership experts agree that character, or integrity, is foundational to business and leadership success.

Both secular and Christian leaders realize that integrity must be paramount in the life of a leader. The dictionary definition of integrity is: "A firm attachment to moral or artistic principle; honesty and sincerity; uprightness; wholeness, completeness; the condition of being unmarred or uncorrupted, the original, perfect condition." Integrity means being consistent in one's behavior under every circumstance, including those unguarded moments. If leaders are normally peaceable and well mannered, but they throw violent temper tantrums when things go wrong, their lives lack integrity. If leaders are honest and moral in public, but discard those standards in private, their lives lack integrity. When leaders have integrity, their followers always know what to expect.

The Bible also uses the term "blameless" to describe integrity. The apostle Peter urged Christians, in light of Christ's second coming to "be diligent to be found by Him in peace, spotless and blameless" (2 Pet. 3:14).

Read the scriptural promises in the margin about integrity. What do you sense God is saying to you about your character?_____

In what area of your character are you vulnerable to compromise your integrity? _____

_____

_____

_____

_____

SCRIPTURE

"He stores up sound wisdom for the upright; he is a shield to those who walk in integrity" (Prov. 2:7, NASB).

"He who walks in integrity walks securely, but he who perverts his ways will be found out" (Prov. 10:9, NASB).

"A righteous man who walks in his integrity— how blessed are his sons after him" (Prov. 20:7, NASB).

"Vindicate me, O LORD, for I have walked in my integrity, And I have trusted in the Lord without wavering. Examine me, O LORD, and try me; Test my mind and my heart" (Ps. 26:1-2, NASB).

Why is a leader's personal life so important? Some people claim leaders who commit adultery can still lead their organizations effectively. They argue that one matter does not affect the other. The issue, however, is integrity. If a man can deceive his wife and children, break a vow he made to God in the presence of witnesses, and knowingly betray the trust of those who love him, what guarantee does his organization have that he will be honest in his dealings with them? People who prove themselves deceitful in one area of life are equally capable of being deceitful in other areas. Perhaps that is why when Warren Bennis and Burt Nanus surveyed sixty successful CEOs of major companies, almost all of them were still married to their first spouse.[3] These leaders valued their commitments and were living their married lives, as well as their business lives, with integrity.

People who prove themselves deceitful in one area of life are equally capable of being deceitful in other areas.

An unmistakable sense of authority accompanies leaders with integrity. Leaders without integrity may promote worthwhile causes yet fail to gain people's loyalty because their lives discredit the validity of their proposals. When people live lives of integrity, their followers assume they are trustworthy to lead. Leaders who are not haphazard with their own lifestyles will be trusted to not be careless with their organizations.

Integrity alone is not sufficient to ensure successful leadership. A leader must also have competence. But integrity will gain a leader the benefit of the doubt from followers who do not yet see the vision as clearly as the leader does.

Integrity is not automatic. It is a character trait that leaders consciously cultivate in their lives. Early in Billy Graham's ministry, he met with his associates during a crusade in Modesto, California. They were troubled by the notorious vices of well-known evangelists and they feared that, if they were not careful, they, too, could fall prey to immorality. Graham led his group to identify those things most likely to destroy or hinder their ministry. Then they agreed upon a list of principles they would each follow in order to ensure the integrity of their lives and their ministry. Graham described this time as "a shared commitment to do all we could to uphold the Bible's standard of absolute integrity and purity for evangelists."[4] As a result of this early commitment to integrity, Billy Graham's evangelistic association became the foremost model of integrity for Christian organizations around the world. Integrity doesn't happen by accident. It happens on purpose.

Integrity is not automatic. It is a character trait that leaders consciously cultivate in their lives.

DAY FIVE

A Legitimate Source of Influence: Preparation

At the close of his autobiography, Billy Graham listed several things he would do differently if he could live his life over again. He said, "I have failed many times, and I would do many things differently. For one thing, I would speak less and study more."[5] Billy Graham preached to more people and saw more conversions than any preacher in history, yet he acknowledged that if he had been better prepared, God might have used his life to an even greater extent!

Preparation brings profound confidence to leaders. Successful leaders invest time in learning the history of their organizations. Spiritual leaders carefully study their organization's past in order to identify the way God has been leading to date. History is particularly important for spiritual leaders new to their churches or organizations. When pastors arrive at churches, they are remiss to assume that God arrives with them! God was there at the church's founding, and He will be there when the pastor leaves. A wise pastor will scrutinize the church's history to see how God has led thus far in order to gain perspective on how God is guiding at present.

Good leaders take time to learn.

Preparation for leadership also involves training. Good leaders take time to learn. Many a zealous leader has charged off to serve the Lord, disdainfully neglecting opportunities to obtain an education or additional skills, only to face issues in their organization that far exceed their expertise. Leaders who make the effort to obtain proper training are not only better prepared for their leadership role; they also have more credibility with those they lead. As the writer of Proverbs extols: "Do you see a man skilled in his work? He will stand before kings; He will not stand before obscure men" (Prov. 22:29).

What is your plan to continue growing personally and mentally? Record your response in the margin.

Not all learning comes through formal education, but a good education must not be discounted as an important means of preparation. The Old Testament leader who towers over the rest is Moses. But before Moses became a leader, he received a good education. He became a thinker, the systematic theologian of the Old Testament. Moses received his formal education from the finest schools in Egypt. His mind had been trained to think. Apart from Jesus, there is no more influential leader in the New Testament than the apostle Paul. He, too, was a thinker, the systematic theologian of the New Testament. Paul earned what today would be considered a Ph.D. in his field, studying under Gamaliel (Acts 22:3), who was considered to be one of the greatest minds of his day.

Whether you are a CEO, a pastor, a school principal, or a committee chairperson, every leader should periodically take a leadership inventory. No matter what leadership capacity you hold, you need to ask yourself these questions: "Why are people following me?" Is it because they are paid to do so? Is it because they can't find a better job? Is it because they believe it is their duty? Or, do they see the activity of God in my life? Do they recognize in my character and integrity the mark of God? Do they sense that God is with me? Do I have a track record of success? If my employees received more lucrative job offers, would they choose to remain with me? What is it about me, if anything, that causes people to want to follow me? Spiritual influence does not come automatically, haphazardly, or easily. It is not something upon which leaders can insist. It is something God must produce in you.

> Spiritual influence does not come automatically, haphazardly, or easily

Concepts for Consideration
- Position, power, and personality are all misconceived sources of influence for leaders.
- Leaders do not have to prove God is guiding them. God's presence will be unmistakable.
- Spiritual leadership flows out of a person's vibrant, intimate relationship with God.
- Character, or integrity, is foundational to leadership success.
- Leaders can make momentous decisions with confidence if they are adequately prepared.

1. H. W. Crocker, Robert E. *Lee on Leadership: Executive Lessons in Character, Courage, and Vision* (Rocklin, Calif.: Forum, 1999), 4.
2. John Pollock, *Moody* (Grand Rapids: Baker Books, 1963), 89.
3. Warren Bennis and Burt Nanus, *Leaders: Strategies for Taking Charge* (New York: HarperCollins, 1997), 24.
4. Billy Graham, *Just as I Am* (New York: HarperCollins, 1997), 150.
5. Ibid., 852.

LEADER GUIDE

Before the Session

1. Make a poster titled: "Legitimate Sources of Influence." Beneath the title, list the four legitimate sources of influence: "God's Authentication," "Encounters with God," "Character/Integrity," and "Preparation."

2. Enlist a learner to present a brief summary, based on the material on page 60, of Moses' being a leader who was affirmed by God.

3. Enlist a learner to present a brief summary of Paul's conversion experience as described in Acts 9:3-19; 22:6-21; 26:13-23.

During the Session

1. State that this is the fifth week in a six-week study of leadership. Begin the session by asking the question: *What is the difference between being a character and having character?* After a brief discussion, point to the poster with the lesson's title and say that today's lesson will focus on the leader's character.

2. Remind learners that in the September 11 lesson we learned that the spiritual leader's task is to move people from where they are to where God wants them to be (p. 23). This is influence. Describe a person who has influenced you. State that we all have similar examples of those who have influenced us both negatively and positively. Divide the class into several small groups and direct individuals in the group to share about persons of influence in their lives.

3. Ask: *Whom do you influence? How?* State that influence can come from several sources, some legitimate and other illegitimate. Write a large *P* on the chalkboard. Explain that there are three illegitimate sources of influence—position, power, and personality. After brief explanation, ask for responses to the bolded question on page 60: *What problems might come to leaders who rely only on position, power, or personality to influence others?*

4. Point to the first legitimate source of influence on the poster you created earlier (God's Authentication). Call on the person enlisted earlier to present the example of Moses as one who was affirmed by God. Ask learners to identify the five evidences of God's authentication from page 61. Blackaby contends that one unmistakable mark of leaders who are authenticated by God is that function in a Christlike manner. Call on volunteers to read 1 Thessalonians 1:6; Ephesians 5:1; and 1 Corinthians 11:1. Direct learners to brainstorm Christlike characteristics and to consider whether their lives exemplify these characteristics.☊

5. Point to the second legitimate source of influence on the poster (Encounters with God). Call attention to the quote in the margin of page 62: "You cannot be a spiritual leader if you are not meeting God in profound, life-changing ways." Call on the person enlisted earlier to present the summary of Paul's conversion experience. Ask participants to share personal encounters they have had with God.❤

6. Point to the third legitimate source of influence on the poster (Character/Integrity). Read Blackaby's definition of integrity on page 64: "Integrity means being consistent in one's behavior under every circumstance, including those unguarded moments." Invite learners to share their own definitions of integrity. Ask: *Why is a leader's personal life important?* After allowing time for learners' responses, summarize the first and second paragraphs on page 65. Emphasize that integrity is a character trait that leaders consciously cultivate in their lives. Challenge participants to list ways to cultivate integrity, recording their suggestions on the board.

7. Point to the fourth legitimate source of influence on the poster (Preparation). Briefly describe Moses' and Paul's preparation for leadership (p. 67). Remind learners that not all learning comes through formal education. *What are some ways you can better prepare yourself to lead?*

8. Review by reminding learners that leadership involves influence. Influence may be negative or positive. The sources of our influence on others may be legitimate or illegitimate. Challenge learners to ensure that their influence will be positive for the kingdom of God because their influence finds its legitimate source in God. Close with prayer.

After the Session

Write a letter of thanks to someone who has been a positive influence for Christ in your life. Encourage members of the class to do the same.

The Leader's Goal: Moving People On to God's Agenda

DAY ONE

An Unworthy Goal: Getting Results

When Mel Blackaby, the third son in our family, was a young seminary student, he was delighted to be called as pastor to a small rural church in Texas. His first pastorate! Before long he was required to conduct his first funeral. To his relief, the service went smoothly. Then it was time to drive to the cemetery for the graveside service. Mel was instructed to drive his car at the front of the procession, just behind a police car. Mel had not yet been to the cemetery, but he assumed the policeman would lead the way. The mourners moved slowly forward, forming a line of vehicles a mile long. Mel felt exhilarated to be ministering to such an impressive group of people in his small town. All was well until the procession came to an uncontrolled intersection. The policeman driving the lead car dutifully pulled over and, after waving the bewildered minister forward, stayed behind to direct traffic. Poor Mel was leading a mile-long group of mourners to a place he had never been. He had absolutely no clue where he was going! What should he do? As he tells it, "I drove as slowly as possible hoping that someone would figure out that I didn't know where I was going and come to my rescue!"

Leaders who take on a new position must ask themselves: Where should this organization be going? This question may seem ridiculously simplistic, but it is amazing how many leaders become so focused on the journey they lose sight of the destination.

> It is amazing how many leaders become so focused on the journey they lose sight of the destination.

Which do you think is more important for a leader—the journey or the destination? Or, are they equally important? Explain your answer. _____

_____

_____

Read the parable of the good Samaritan (Luke 10:25-37) and the parable of the rich fool (Luke 12:13-21). How do these parables highlight the perils of focusing exclusively on either the destination or the goal? _____

_____

_____

_____

_____

_____

_____

It's not that these leaders have no agenda for their organization. They may in fact have high aspirations and detailed plans of what they hope to achieve. The problem is that they fail to examine whether these plans will lead them to results that are truly best for their organization. Some leaders confuse the means to the end with the end itself. If leaders do not clearly understand where their organization is and where it should be going, they will be unable to lead effectively.

What do people want to see happen when they choose a new leader? *Results.* It is human nature to look for tangible measures of success. Even in religious circles, people establish goals to measure their organization's success. For example, churches determine their effectiveness by focusing on things they can count: number of seats filled in the auditorium, number of dollars in the offering plate, number of ministries conducted throughout the week. Peter Drucker says the ultimate measure of leadership is "results."[1] Successful leaders must be people who get things done! This demand for measurable results from leaders puts pressure on people to focus on their accomplishments.

The popular trend is to focus entirely on achieving goals. When goals are met, leaders consider themselves successful. But what about the price their organizations pay in achieving the goals? Interestingly, secular writers realize that organizational leadership involves far more than merely reaching goals. Great leaders concentrate on building great organizations. Leaders can achieve their goals for a time but destroy their organizations in the process.

Leaders who strive for and even achieve their goals but whose people suffer and fall by the wayside in the process have failed as leaders. Using people to achieve organizational goals is the antithesis of spiritual leadership. The end does not justify the means in God's kingdom. Getting results can make leaders look good. God's way magnifies God's name.

> The popular trend is to focus entirely on achieving goals.

DAY TWO

An Unworthy Goal:
Bigger, Faster, More

Religious leaders who are able to grow megachurches are treated as spiritual heroes. They are encouraged to write books chronicling their success, and they regularly appear on the speaking circuit for church growth conferences. Even if these leaders fall into immorality, churches may be reluctant to relieve them of their duties because it appears God still has his hand of blessing upon them. We have often heard people ask, "If what our pastor did was so wrong, why has God blessed him so?" This question equates growth with God's blessing. That's not always the case. Certainly church growth is inevitable in a healthy church, as the Book of Acts clearly exemplifies. But it is also entirely possible for a church to grow in numbers apart from God's blessing. There is a significant difference between drawing a crowd and building a church. Marketers can draw a crowd. They can't grow a church. Cults can draw a crowd. They can't build God's

> It is entirely possible for a church to grow in numbers apart from God's blessing.

kingdom. If growth in numbers is a sure sign of God's blessing, then many cult groups are enjoying God's blessing to a far greater extent than many churches.

Explain the difference between drawing a crowd and growing a church. _____

_____

_____

_____

_____

There is a significant difference between drawing a crowd and building a church.

The seduction is in believing that God is as impressed with crowds as people are. He is not. The essence of Satan's temptations for Jesus was trying to convince Him to draw a crowd rather than build a church (Matt. 4). When Jesus fed the 5,000, He became so popular that the people wanted to forcibly make Him their king. In response, Jesus began teaching them about true discipleship. Jesus knew that, even though there was a large crowd following Him, many of them were not believers. They were simply wanting their physical needs met. So Jesus preached to them about the cost of discipleship. "As a result of this many of His disciples withdrew, and were not walking with Him anymore" (John 6:66). So quick and so vast was the exodus of would-be disciples that Jesus turned to the Twelve and asked if they, too, intended to abandon Him (v. 67). Jesus was never enamored with crowds. In fact, He often sought to escape them (Mark 1:35-38).

Read John 6:60-71. How does this experience underscore the fact that crowds were not Jesus' ultimate goal? _____

_____

_____

_____

Churches often use the world's methods to draw a crowd. A grand performance done with excellence, using high-tech sound equipment, professional lighting, eye-catching brochures, and charismatic leadership, can draw a crowd. It will not, however, build a church. Only Christ can do that. Does this mean that churches should not seek to do the best they can? Should churches never compose attractive brochures or invest in quality sound and lighting equipment? Of course they should. But leaders must be diligent that they never shift their trust from the Head of the church to the tools of the world. They should never assume that, because attendance is growing, their church is healthy and pleasing to God. Leaders must continuously measure their success by God's standards and not by the world's.

Read Matthew 16:18 and Ephesians 2:19-22. What important truths do these Scriptures teach about God's church? _____

_____

_____

_____

DAY THREE

A Worthy Goal: Leading to Spiritual Maturity

SCRIPTURE

"You have seen what I did to the Egyptians and how I carried you on eagles' wings and brought you to Me" (Ex. 19:4, HCSB).

Assuming leaders do not succumb to misguided goals for their organizations, what should their goals be? There are at least three legitimate goals spiritual leaders ought to have for their people regardless of whether they are leading a committee, a church, or a corporation.

The ultimate goal of spiritual leadership is not to achieve numerical results alone, or to do things with perfection, or even to grow for the sake of growth. It is to take their people from where they are to where God wants them to be. God's primary concern for all people is not results, but relationship. People's call to be in a right relationship with God takes precedence over their occupation. Calling comes *before* vocation. There is a profound comment on this issue in Exodus 19:4: "You yourselves have seen what I did to the Egyptians, and how I bore you on eagles' wings, and brought you to Myself."

At first glance, this verse can seem confusing. It refers to the Israelites who were rescued from slavery in Egypt. We tend to assume that God delivered the Israelites so that He could bring them to the Promised Land in Canaan. But that is not what God said. The key for God was not the *region* but the *relationship*. God delivered the Israelites so they could be free to develop an intimate relationship with Him, a relationship of faith and obedience. The location was simply a means for that relationship to be developed. The reason the Israelites spent 40 futile years wandering in the wilderness was not that God could not give them victory in Canaan. He could have easily done that. However, God took them into the wilderness for 40 years in order to establish a proper relationship with them. The place was accessible, but the relationship was not yet where God wanted it to be. Unfortunately, once the Israelites entered the Promised Land, they came to see the land as an end in itself rather than a means to a relationship with God. As a result, God ultimately took their land away from them.

One of the issues regarding spiritual leadership is whether spiritual leaders can take people to places they themselves have never been. That depends on one's definition of spiritual leadership. If spiritual leadership is understood as taking people to a *location* or completing a *task,* then leaders can lead people to places they have never been. But if the goal of leadership is a *relationship,* then leaders will never move their people beyond where they have gone themselves. Leaders can lead people to relocate their organization or to build a building or to grow in size without prior experience in these areas. But leaders cannot take their people into a relationship with Christ that goes any deeper than they have gone themselves. Followers may grow deeper spiritually in spite of their spiritually immature leaders, but they will not grow deeper because of such people. Thus, spiritual leaders must continually be growing themselves if they are to lead their people into a mature, intimate relationship with Christ. Leaders will not lead their people to higher levels of prayer unless they have already ascended to those heights themselves. Leaders will not lead others to deeper levels of trust in God unless they have a mature faith themselves.

> Leaders cannot take their people into a relationship with Christ that goes any deeper than they have gone themselves.

A spiritual organization will reach its maximum potential only when every member knows how to hear clearly from God and is willing to respond in obedience. It is not enough for leaders to hear from God and then relay the message to the people. Each believer must learn to recognize God's voice and understand what He is saying. When this is true of an organization, leaders will not need to "sell" their visions; they will simply share with their people what God has said to them and then allow their people to seek confirmation themselves.

What are you currently doing to grow spiritually? _____

_____

_____

_____

What additional steps can you take to grow spiritually? _____

_____

_____

_____

DAY FOUR

A Worthy Goal: Leading Others to Lead

> One of the most tragic mistakes leaders commit is to make themselves indispensable.

Leaders lead followers. Great leaders lead leaders. One of the most tragic mistakes leaders commit is to make themselves indispensable. Sometimes insecurity can drive people to hoard all the leadership opportunities for themselves so that no one else appears as capable or as successful. Other times leaders get so caught up in their own work that they fail to invest time in developing other leaders in the organization. If some leaders were to be completely honest, they would acknowledge that they enjoy being indispensable. They like being the only person in the organizational lime-light. Failing to develop leaders in an organization is tantamount to gross failure by the leader, whether by design or by neglect.

One of the most common failures of leaders is that they spend little time or effort preparing their organization for their departure. Many leaders work extremely hard at their jobs, and they may enjoy remarkable success during their term as leader. But one test of great leaders is how well their organizations do after they leave. This phenomenon can be clearly seen in the life of Samuel. Samuel was one of the most godly leaders Israel ever had. At the time of his "retirement," no one with whom he had worked could find any fault with him (1 Sam. 12:1-5). Nevertheless, Samuel ultimately failed as a leader, for he did not prepare a successor.

"And it came about when Samuel was old that he appointed his sons judges over Israel. Now the name of his first-born was Joel, and the name of his second, Abijah; they were judging in Beersheba. His sons, however, did not walk in his ways, but turned aside after dishonest gain and took bribes and perverted justice.

Then all the elders of Israel gathered together and came to Samuel at Ramah; and they said to him, 'Behold, you have grown old, and your sons do not walk in your ways. Now appoint a king for us to judge us like all the nations.' But the thing was displeasing in the sight of Samuel when they said, 'Give us a king to judge us.' And Samuel prayed to the Lord" (1 Sam. 8:1-6).

Samuel failed on two counts: as a parent and as a leader. As long as the Israelites had the noble Samuel for their leader, they followed him without protest. But when Samuel became older and appointed his sons, Joel and Abijah, to replace him, the Israelites resisted. Later generations have castigated the Israelites for rejecting God's leadership at this time and asking for a king. The fact is, the spiritual leaders available to them were so inferior that they saw a secular king as a preferable option. If Samuel had groomed an acceptable replacement, the people might not have clamored for a king. The people's failure stemmed from their leader's failure to do his job.

Samuel's mistake was very costly but, sadly, very common as well. Samuel's example demonstrates that a leader's failure carries with it significant ramifications for everyone in the organization, present members and future members alike. Developing leaders must be a core value of any leader. Unless leaders are intentional about developing leaders within their organization, it will not happen.

Whom are you presently developing as an emerging leader? ___

_____

_____

DAY FIVE

A Worthy Goal:
Bringing Glory to God

There is a third goal leaders should have for their organizations, one which is the ultimate goal of any organization and the reason behind the first two goals of leadership—to bring God glory. Whether people lead Christian or secular organizations, their goal ought to be to glorify God by the way they lead their organization. Christian organizations affirm their desire to glorify God, but they can become sidetracked in many subtle ways. Churches can become so preoccupied with growing in numbers or erecting buildings or running programs that they incorrectly assume that everything they are doing honors God. While Christians regularly give lip service to their desire to glorify God, not everything they do necessarily accomplishes this goal. God is not concerned with bringing glory to people. He wants to reveal His glory through people. Christian organizations do not do this spontaneously. It is the leader's goal to keep this task at the forefront of their organization's agenda. A leader's assignments and positions will change over time, but the goal of bringing glory to God must always be the impetus behind the efforts of every Christian.

> Churches can become so preoccupied with growing in numbers or erecting buildings or running programs that they incorrectly assume that everything they are doing honors God.

Describe the difference between bringing glory to people and God revealing His glory through people. _____

_____

_____

_____

_____

Bringing glory to God is not complicated. People bring God glory when they reveal God's nature to a watching world. When Christian leaders forgive others, people come to understand that God is a God who forgives. When Christian leaders are patient with those who fail, people come to understand that God is, by nature, long-suffering. When Christian leaders live with holy integrity, people gain a glimpse of God's holiness. The first glimpse of the true God that many people see will be reflected in the Christians who work alongside them week by week. To accurately reflect God's nature to others is to bring Him glory.

God has a specific agenda for every person and every organization. Leaders can only discover God's will as He reveals it to them through their personal relationship with Him. There are, however, spiritual goals that should guide every leader. Bringing people to spiritual maturity, developing leaders and, most importantly, bringing glory to God ought to be basic objectives of every leader.

Read John 8:50 and fill in the blank: Even _____ did not seek glory for Himself but for _____.

Read 1 Corinthians 10:31 and fill in the blank: God's glory can be revealed through our_____ .

Read 1 Peter 4:13 and fill in the blank: God's glory can be revealed through our _____ .

How does your life bring glory to God?_____
_____
_____
_____

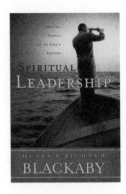

Henry and Richard Blackaby's book, *Spiritual Leadership*, contains additional material not included in this *Masterwork* study. If you would like to read and study this book in greater detail, you can obtain your own copy of *Spiritual Leadership* by visiting the LifeWay Christian Store serving you, or by calling 1-800-458-2772.

Concepts for Consideration

• Leaders can achieve their goals and yet be out of God's will. Reaching goals is not necessarily a sign of God's blessing.

• In God's eyes, how something is done is as important as what is done. The end does not justify the means in God's kingdom.

• There is a significant difference between drawing a crowd and building a church. Marketers can draw a crowd. Cults can draw a crowd. They can't build God's kingdom.

• One of the issues regarding spiritual leadership is whether spiritual leaders can take people to places they themselves have never been.

• God is not concerned with bringing glory to people. He wants to reveal His glory through people.

1. Peter F. Drucker, foreword to *The Leader of the Future*, edited by Francis Hasselbein, Marshall Goldsmith, and Richard Beckhard (San Francisco: Jossey Bass, 1996), xii.

LEADER GUIDE

Before the Session

1. Enlist two learners to prepare to discuss in class two parables: the parable of the good Samaritan (Luke 10:25-37) and the parable of the rich fool (Luke 12:13-21).

2. Make a sentence-strip poster with the statement: "Leaders must continuously measure their success by God's standards and not by the world's."

3. Write the following on a poster board or whiteboard: "Worthy Goals of Spiritual Leadership."

During the Session

1. Ask the question: *Which is more important—the journey or the destination? Why? What happens when leaders become so focused on the journey that they lose sight of the destination? What happens when leaders become so focused on the destination that they pay little attention to the journey?* (See material in Day One.) After a brief discussion exploring the perils of focusing on one to the exclusion of the other, call on the learners enlisted to highlight these perils as taught by Jesus in the parables of the good Samaritan and rich fool. Describe how Jesus focused on both His destination and journey.

2. Call on readers to read the sentence-strip poster in unison: "Leaders must continuously measure their success by God's standards and not by the world's." Ask learners to list worldly standards that may distract churches and church leaders from God's standards. In Day Two Blackaby stated that a church can "grow in numbers apart from God's blessings" (p. 72). Ask learners if they agree or disagree. Ask: *What's the difference between drawing a crowd and growing a church?* Call on a volunteer to read John 6:60-71. Then ask: *How does this passage shed light on the subject?*

3. Ask: *What did Blackaby identify as the ultimate goal of spiritual leadership?* The ultimate goal of spiritual leadership is to take people from where they are to where God wants them to be (p. 74). Write "Leading to Spiritual Maturity" on the Worthy Goals poster. Call on a volunteer to read Exodus 19:4. Ask: *According to this verse, why did God deliver the Israelites from slavery in Egypt?* (to bring them to Himself) Emphasize that the key was not the *region* but the *relationship*. (See the first full paragraph on page 75.) State that once the Israelites entered the Promised Land, they came to see the land as an end in itself rather than a means to a relationship with God. Ask: *Do we likewise at times confuse the means with the end? Explain.* Call attention to the quote in margin of page 75. Lead learners to list ways they can grow spiritually.◉

4. Ask: *What do you think is the difference between a leader and a great leader?* Allow for discussion, then suggest that one difference is great leaders lead others to lead. Write on the poster: "Leading Others to Lead." Ask learners to recall how Blackaby described the difference between leaders and great leaders. Using the material on page 77, explain how Samuel missed out on the opportunity to be a great leader. Encourage participants to seek opportunities to discover and respond to opportunities to train tomorrow's leaders.◐

5. State that there is a third goal leaders should have—to bring glory to God. Write on the poster: "Bringing Glory to God." Ask: *How can we bring glory to God?* After brief discussion, point out that Blackaby wrote that we bring glory to God by revealing His nature to others. Ask for examples of how we can do that. Call on volunteers to read 1 Corinthians 10:31 and 1 Peter 4:13 and say that we can bring glory to God through our daily activities and our suffering.

6. Review the Concepts for Consideration on page 79. Ask: *Is there one of these concepts that has caused you to think of spiritual leadership in a different way?* Close in prayer, asking God to develop, guide, and empower participants to be the leaders He wants them to be.

After the Session
Continue to encourage learners to identify and respond affirmatively to leadership opportunities God may bring to them.

ABOUT THE WRITERS

RANDY
ALCORN

is the founder and director of Eternal Perspective Ministries (EPM), a nonprofit ministry devoted to promoting an eternal viewpoint and drawing attention to people in special need of advocacy and help. A pastor for fourteen years before founding EPM in 1990, Randy is a popular teacher and conference speaker, and has authored numerous books.

AMY
SUMMERS

wrote the personal learning activites and teaching plans. Amy is a graduate of Baylor University and Southwestern Baptist Theological Seminary. She lives in Arden, North Carolina.

Heaven

In 1952, young Florence Chadwick stepped into the waters of the Pacific Ocean off Catalina Island, determined to swim to the shore of mainland California. She'd already been the first woman to swim the English Channel both ways. The weather was foggy and chilly; she could hardly see the boats accompanying her. Still, she swam for fifteen hours. When she begged to be taken out of the water along the way, her mother, in a boat alongside, told her she was close and that she could make it. Finally, physically and emotionally exhausted, she stopped swimming and was pulled out. It wasn't until she was on the boat that she discovered the shore was less than half a mile away. At a news conference the next day she said, "All I could see was the fog.... I think if I could have seen the shore, I would have made it."

Consider her words: "I think if I could have seen the shore, I would have made it." For believers, that shore is Jesus and being with Him in the place that He promised to prepare for us, where we will live with Him forever. The shore we should look for is that of the New Earth. If we can see through the fog and picture our eternal home in our mind's eye, it will comfort and energize us.

If you're weary and don't know how you can keep going, I pray this study will give you vision, encouragement, and hope. No matter how tough life gets, if you can see the shore and draw your strength from Christ, you'll make it.

I pray this study will help you see the shore.

—RANDY ALCORN

Realizing Our Destiny

DAY ONE

Are You Looking Forward to Heaven?

Read Colossians 3:1-2 in your Bible and fill in the blanks:

Believers are to set their _____ and _____on _____ and not on _____.

Jonathan Edwards, the great Puritan preacher, often spoke of Heaven.[1] He said, "It becomes us to spend this life only as a journey toward heaven ... to which we should subordinate all other concerns of life. Why should we labor for or set our hearts on anything else, but that which is our proper end and true happiness?"[2]

In his early twenties, Edwards composed a set of life resolutions. One read, "Resolved, to endeavor to obtain for myself as much happiness, in the other world, as I possibly can."[3]

Some may think it odd and inappropriate that Edwards was so committed to pursuing happiness for himself in Heaven. If we all seek happiness, why not do as Edwards did and seek it where it can actually be found—in the person of Jesus and the place called Heaven?

Tragically, however, most people do not find their joy in Christ and Heaven. In fact, many people find no joy at all when they think about Heaven.

> "It becomes us to spend this life only as a journey toward heaven ... to which we should subordinate all other concerns of life."
> – Jonathan Edwards

∽

SCRIPTURE

"For me, living is Christ and dying is gain. Now if I live on in the flesh, this means fruitful work for me; and I don't know which one I should choose. I am pressured by both. I have the desire to depart and be with Christ—which is far better" (Phil. 1:21-23, HCSB).

A pastor once confessed to me, "Whenever I think about Heaven, it makes me depressed. I'd rather just cease to exist when I die."

"Why?" I asked.

"I can't stand the thought of that endless tedium. To float around in the clouds with nothing to do but strum a harp … it's all so terribly boring. Heaven doesn't sound much better than Hell. I'd rather be annihilated than spend eternity in a place like that."

Where did this Bible-believing, seminary-educated pastor get such a view of Heaven? Certainly not from Scripture, where Paul said to depart and be with Christ was far better than staying on a sin-cursed earth (Phil. 1:23). My friend was more honest about it than most, yet I've found that many Christians share the same misconceptions about Heaven.

If you honestly compared your concept of Heaven to this pastor's, would it be THE SAME or DIFFERENT? (Circle your answer.) Briefly explain. _____

_____

_____

_____

_____

I believe there's one central explanation for why so many of God's children have such a vague, negative, and uninspired view of Heaven: the work of Satan.

Jesus said of the Devil, "When he lies, he speaks his native language, for he is a liar and the father of lies" (John 8:44). Some of Satan's favorite lies are about Heaven. Revelation 13:6 tells us the satanic beast "opened his mouth to blaspheme God, and to slander his name and his dwelling place and those who live in heaven." Our enemy slanders three things: God's Person, God's people, and God's place—namely, Heaven.

Our enemy slanders three things: God's Person, God's people, and God's place— namely, Heaven.

After being forcibly evicted from Heaven (Isa. 14:12-15), the Devil became bitter not only toward God, but toward mankind and toward Heaven itself, the place that was no longer his. It must be maddening for him that we're now entitled to the home he was kicked out of. What better way for the devil and his demons to attack us than to whisper lies about the very place on which God tells us to set our hearts and minds?

Satan need not convince us that Heaven doesn't exist. He need only convince us that Heaven is a place of boring, unearthly existence. If we believe that lie, we'll be robbed of our joy and anticipation, we'll set our minds on this life and not the next, and we won't be motivated to share our faith. Why should we share the "good news" that people can spend eternity in a boring, ghostly place that even we're not looking forward to?

Because Satan hates us, he's determined to rob us of the joy we'd have if we believed what God tells us about the magnificent world to come.

> Satan need not convince us that Heaven doesn't exist. He need only convince us that Heaven is a place of boring, unearthly existence.

DAY TWO

Is Heaven Beyond Our Imagination?

When Marco Polo returned to Italy from the court of Kublai Khan, he described a world his audience had never seen—one that could not be understood without the eyes of imagination. Not that China was an imaginary realm, but it was very different from Italy. Yet as two locations on planet Earth inhabited by human beings, they had much in common. The reference points of Italy allowed a basis for understanding China, and the differences could be spelled out from there.[4]

The writers of Scripture present Heaven in many ways. Read the following passages in your Bible and state some of those ways:

Hebrews 11:16 _____

_____

Revelation 19:9 _____

_____

Revelation 21:2 _____

_____

Revelation 22:1-2 _____

_____

Because gardens, cities, and kingdoms are familiar to us, they afford us a bridge to understanding Heaven. However, many people make the mistake of assuming that these are merely analogies with no actual correspondence to the reality of Heaven (which would make them poor analogies). Analogies can be pressed too far, but because Scripture makes it clear that Jesus is preparing a place for us, and God's kingdom will come to earth, and a physical resurrection awaits us, there is no reason to spiritualize or allegorize all earthly descriptions of Heaven. Indeed, some of them may be simple, factual statements.

A pastor visiting my office asked what I was writing. "A big book on Heaven," I said.

"Well," he replied, "since Scripture says 'No eye has seen, no ear has heard, no mind has conceived what God has prepared for those who love him,' what will you be talking about? Obviously, we can't know what God has prepared for us in Heaven." (He was referring to 1 Cor. 2:9.)

I said to him what I always say: "You didn't complete the sentence. You also have to read verse 10." Here's how the complete sentence reads: "'No eye has seen, no ear has heard, no mind has conceived what God has prepared for those who love him'—but God has revealed it to us by his Spirit." The context makes it clear that this revelation is God's Word (v. 13), which tells us what God has prepared for us.

God has explained to us what Heaven is like. Not exhaustively, but accurately.

What we otherwise could not have known about Heaven, because we're unable to see it, God says He has revealed to us through His Spirit. This means that God has explained to us what Heaven is like. Not exhaustively, but accurately. God tells us about Heaven in His Word, not so we can shrug our shoulders and remain ignorant, but because He wants us to understand and anticipate what awaits us.

Other verses are likewise pulled out to derail discussions about Heaven. For example, "The secret things belong to the Lord our God" (Deut. 29:29). Heaven is regarded as a "secret thing." But the rest of the verse—again, rarely quoted—completes the thought: "But the things revealed belong to us and to our children forever."

We should accept that many things about Heaven are secret and that God has countless surprises in store for us. But as for the things God has revealed to us about Heaven, these things belong to us and to our children. It's critically important that we study and understand them. That is precisely why God revealed them to us!

Another "silencer" is 2 Corinthians 12:2-4. Paul says that 14 years earlier he was "caught up to paradise," where he "heard inexpressible things, things that man is not permitted to tell." Some people use this verse to say we should not discuss what Heaven will be like. But all it says is that God didn't permit Paul to talk about his visit to Heaven. In contrast, God commanded the apostle John to talk about his prolonged visit to Heaven, which he did in detail in the Book of Revelation. Likewise, Isaiah and Ezekiel wrote about what they saw in Heaven.

Although it's inappropriate for us to speculate on what Paul might have seen in Heaven, it's certainly appropriate to discuss what John saw, because God chose to reveal it to us. If He didn't intend for us to understand it, why would He bother telling us about it? So, we should study, teach, and discuss God's revelation about Heaven given to us in His Word.

Isaiah 55:9 is another verse often cited in support of a "don't ask, don't tell" approach to Heaven: "As the heavens are higher than the earth, so are my ways higher than your ways and my thoughts than your thoughts." God's thoughts are indeed higher than ours, but when He reduces His thoughts into words and reveals them in Scripture, He expects us to study them, meditate on them, and understand them—again, not exhaustively, but accurately.

Ask God to remove the blinders of your preconceived ideas about Heaven so you can understand what He has revealed about Heaven in Scripture. You may desire to use the Scriptural prayers in the margin.

Lord, give me the discipline to reflect on what Your Word is saying about Heaven. Give me insight beyond what I can grasp on my own (2 Tim. 2:7).

Open my eyes so I can see wonderful things in Your Word (Ps. 119:18) about the place You have prepared for me.

DAY THREE

Is Heaven Our Default Destination?

For every American who believes he's going to Hell, there are 120 who believe they're going to Heaven.[5]

SCRIPTURE

"Enter through the
narrow gate. For wide
is the gate and broad is
the road that leads to
destruction, and many
enter through it. But
small is the gate and
narrow the road that
leads to life, and only
a few find it" (Matt.
7:13-14, NIV).

Based on Jesus' words in Matthew 7:13-14 (in the margin), is this a false optimism?   YES   NO   NOT SURE

Explain your answer. _____

_____

_____

_____

_____

_____

Heaven is not our
default destination.
No one goes there
automatically.

What would keep us out of Heaven is universal: "All have sinned and fall short of the glory of God" (Rom. 3:23). Sin separates us from a relationship with God (Isa. 59:2). God is so holy that He cannot allow sin into His presence: "Your eyes are too pure to look on evil; you cannot tolerate wrong" (Hab. 1:13). Because we are sinners, we are not entitled to enter God's presence. We cannot enter Heaven as we are.

So Heaven is not our default destination. No one goes there automatically. Unless our sin problem is resolved, the only place we will go is our true default destination … Hell.

I am addressing this issue now because throughout this book I will talk about being with Jesus in Heaven, being reunited with family and friends, and enjoying great adventures in Heaven. The great danger is that readers will assume they are headed for Heaven. Judging by what's said at most funerals, you'd think nearly everyone's going to Heaven, wouldn't you? But Jesus made it clear that most people are not going to Heaven: "But small is the gate and narrow the road that leads to life, and only a few find it" (Matt. 7:14).

Hell will be inhabited by people who haven't received God's gift of redemption in Christ (Rev. 20:12-15). After Christ returns, there will be a resurrection of believers for eternal life in Heaven and a resurrection of unbelievers for eternal existence in Hell (John 5:28-29). The unsaved—everyone whose name is not written in the Lamb's book of life—will be judged by God according to the works they have done, which have been recorded in Heaven's books (Rev. 20:12-15). Because those works include sin, people on their own, without Christ, cannot enter the presence of a holy and just God and will be consigned to a place of everlasting destruction (Matt. 13:40-42). Christ will say to those who are not covered by His blood, "Depart from me, you who are cursed, into the eternal fire prepared for the devil and his angels" (Matt. 25:41).

Many imagine that it is civilized, humane, and compassionate to deny the existence of an eternal Hell, but in fact it is arrogant that we, as creatures, would dare to take what we think is the moral high ground in opposition to what God the Creator has clearly revealed. We don't want to believe that any others deserve eternal punishment, because if they do, so do we. But if we understood God's nature and ours, we would be shocked not that some people could go to Hell (where else would sinners go?), but that any would be permitted into Heaven. By denying the endlessness of Hell, we minimize Christ's work on the cross. Why? Because we lower the stakes of redemption. If Christ's crucifixion and resurrection didn't deliver us from an eternal Hell, His work on the cross is less heroic, less potent, less consequential, and thus less deserving of our worship and praise.

In the Bible, Jesus says more than anyone else about Hell.

Read Matthew 13:41-42, 25:46 and Mark 9:47-48 in the margin and complete this sentence:
Hell is a place of _____
_____
_____
_____
_____ .

Jesus refers to Hell as a literal place and describes it in graphic terms—including raging fires and the worm that doesn't die. Christ says the unsaved "will be thrown outside, into the darkness, where there will be weeping and gnashing of teeth" (Matt. 8:12). In his story of the rich man and Lazarus, Jesus taught that in Hell, the wicked suffer terribly, are fully conscious, retain their desires and memories and reasoning, long for relief, cannot be comforted, cannot leave their torment, and are bereft of hope (Luke 16:19-31). The Savior could not have painted a more bleak or graphic picture.

But is it really possible to know you will go to Heaven when you die? Before diving further into the subject of Heaven, we'll address this question in the next section.

SCRIPTURE

"The Son of Man will send out His angels, and they will gather from His kingdom everything that causes sin and those guilty of lawlessness. They will throw them into the blazing furnace where there will be weeping and gnashing of teeth" (Matt. 13:41-42, HCSB).

"And they will go away into eternal punishment, but the righteous into eternal life" (Matt. 25:46, HCSB).

"And if your eye causes your downfall, gouge it out. It is better for you to enter the kingdom of God with one eye than to have two eyes and be thrown into hell, where Their worm does not die, and the fire is not quenched" (Mark 9:47-48, HCSB).

DAY FOUR

Can You Know You're Going to Heaven?

Ancient cities kept rolls of their citizens. Guards were posted at the city gates to keep out criminals and enemies by checking their names against the list. This is the context for Revelation 21:27: "Nothing impure will ever enter [the city], nor will anyone who does what is shameful or deceitful, but only those whose names are written in the Lamb's book of life."

Many assume that the good they've done—perhaps attending church, being baptized, singing in the choir, or helping in a soup kitchen—will be enough to gain entry to Heaven. But people who do not respond to Christ's invitation to forgive their sins are people whose names aren't written in the Lamb's book of life. To be denied entrance to Heaven means being cast outside into Hell, forever.

In that day, no explanation or excuse will count. All that will matter is whether our names are written in the book. If they're not, we'll be turned away.

SCRIPTURE

"You don't even know what tomorrow will bring—what your life will be! For you are like smoke that appears for a little while, then vanishes" (Jas. 4:14, HCSB).

"Look, now is the acceptable time; now is the day of salvation" (2 Cor. 6:2, HCSB).

Have you said yes to Christ's invitation to spend eternity with Him in His house?   YES   NO

If so, you have reason to rejoice—Heaven's gates will be open to you.

If you have been putting off your response, or if you presume that you can enter Heaven without responding to Christ's invitation, one day you will deeply regret it.

Read James 4:14 and 2 Corinthians 6:2 in the margin. Why is it essential you not wait another minute to respond positively to Christ's invitation and have your name written in His book of life?_____

_____

Turn to the inside front cover of this publication to make today your day of salvation.

Can we really know in advance where we're going when we die? The apostle John, the same one who wrote about the new Heavens and New Earth, said in one of his letters, "I write these things to you who believe in the name of the Son of God so that you may know that you have eternal life" (1 John 5:13). We can know for sure that we have eternal life. We can know for sure that we will go to Heaven when we die.

> We can know for sure that we will go to Heaven when we die.

Do you?

Because of Jesus Christ's sacrificial death on the cross on our behalf, God freely offers us forgiveness. But forgiveness is not automatic. If we want to be forgiven, we must recognize and repent of our sins. Forgiveness is established by our confession: "If we confess our sins, he is faithful and just and will forgive us our sins and purify us from all unrighteousness" (1 John 1:9).

Christ offers to everyone the gift of forgiveness, salvation, and eternal life: "Whoever is thirsty, let him come; and whoever wishes, let him take the free gift of the water of life" (Rev. 22:17).

There's no righteous deed we can do that will earn us a place in Heaven (Titus 3:5). We come to Christ empty-handed. We can take no credit for salvation: "For it is by grace you have been saved, through faith—and this not from yourselves, it is the gift of God—not by works, so that no one can boast" (Eph. 2:8-9).

This gift cannot be worked for, earned, or achieved in any sense. It's not dependent on our merit or effort but solely on Christ's generous and sufficient sacrifice on our behalf. Ultimately, God's greatest gift is Himself. We don't just need salvation, we need Jesus the Savior. It is the Person, God, who graciously gives us the place, Heaven.

To those who presumed they would go to Heaven because they were religious, Jesus said, "Not everyone who says to me, 'Lord, Lord,' will enter the kingdom of heaven, but only he who does the will of my Father who is in heaven. Many will say to me on that day, 'Lord, Lord, did we not prophesy in your name, and in your name drive out demons and perform many miracles?' Then I will tell them plainly, 'I never knew you. Away from me, you evildoers!'" (Matt. 7:21-23). Those who assume their religious activities alone will get them to Heaven have a terrible surprise ahead.

Do not merely assume that you are a Christian and are going to Heaven. Make the conscious decision to accept Christ's sacrificial death on your behalf. When you choose to accept Christ and surrender control of your life to Him, you can be certain that your name is written in the Lamb's book of life.

Do you know for certain you are going to Heaven when you die?
Yes   No
Spend time talking with God and perhaps a trusted Christian adviser about your response.

DAY FIVE

Water for the Thirsty

What are people thirsty for? _____

_____

_____

SCRIPTURE

"And He said to me, 'It is done! I am the Alpha and the Omega, the Beginning and the End. I will give water as a gift to the thirsty from the spring of life'" (Rev. 21:6, HCSB).

After showing us the new Heavens and New Earth, Jesus says near the end of the Bible, "I am the Alpha and the Omega, the Beginning and the End. To him who is thirsty I will give to drink without cost from the spring of the water of life" (Rev. 21:6). But then Jesus adds these sobering words: "He who overcomes will inherit all this, and I will be his God and he will be my son. But the cowardly, the unbelieving, the vile, the murderers, the sexually immoral, those who practice magic arts, the idolaters and all liars—their place will be in the fiery lake of burning sulfur" (Rev. 21:7-8).

For those who know Christ, their place is Heaven. For those who do not know Christ, their place is Hell. Jesus said, "I am the way and the truth and the life. No one comes to the Father except through me" (John 14:6). There is no middle ground. Either you are a follower of Jesus or you are not. Christ said, "He who is not with me is against me" (Luke 11:23).

The Bible ends with yet one more invitation, suggesting that God wants to give every reader one last chance: "The Spirit and the bride say, 'Come!' And let him who hears say, 'Come!' Whoever is thirsty, let him come; and whoever wishes, let him take the free gift of the water of life" (Rev. 22:17). It is Jesus—and Heaven—we thirst for. Jesus and Heaven are offered to us at no cost because He already paid the price for us.

Look back at Revelation 22:17 and underline who issues the invitation to the thirsty to come enjoy Heaven. How is your church, the bride of Christ, issuing that invitation? _____

_____

_____

_____

How can you invite others to enjoy Heaven?_____

_____

_____

_____

Why would you not come? What reason could be good enough to turn away from Jesus and from eternal life in the new Heavens and New Earth? In the words of C. S. Lewis, "All your life an unattainable ecstasy has hovered just beyond the grasp of your consciousness. The day is coming when you will wake to find, beyond all hope, that you have attained it, or else, that it was within your reach and you have lost it forever."[6]

You are made for a Person and a place. Jesus is the Person. Heaven is the place. They are a package—you cannot get Heaven without Jesus or Jesus without Heaven. We will explore Heaven's joys and wonders throughout this study. But we dare not presume we can enter Heaven apart from Christ.

"Seek the Lord while he may be found; call on him while he is near" (Isa. 55:6).

Have you confessed your sins? Have you asked Christ to forgive you? Have you placed your trust in Christ's death and resurrection on your behalf? Have you asked Jesus to be your Lord and empower you to follow Him?

Wouldn't it be tragic if you read this study on Heaven but didn't get to go there?

SCRIPTURE

"Both the Spirit and the bride say, 'Come!' Anyone who hears should say, 'Come!' And the one who is thirsty should come. Whoever desires should take the living water as a gift" (Rev. 22:17, HCSB).

1. To emphasize that Heaven, the New Earth, and Hell are real places, these terms are deliberately capitalized throughout this study, as we would with other proper nouns, such as Chicago, Europe, or Saturn.
2. Ola Elizabeth Winslow, *Jonathan Edwards: Basic Writings* (New York: New American Library, 1966), 142.
3. Jonathan Edwards, "The Resolutions of Jonathan Edwards (1722–23)," JonathanEdwards.com, *http://www.jonathanedwards.com/text/Personal/resolut.htm*; see also Stephen Nichols, ed., *Jonathan Edwards' Resolutions and Advice to Young Converts* (Phillipsburg, N.J.: Presbyterian and Reformed, 2001).
4. Alister E. McGrath, *A Brief History of Heaven* (Malden, Mass.: Blackwell, 2003), 5.
5. K. Connie Kang, "Next Stop, the Pearly Gates . . . or Hell?" *Los Angeles Times*, October 24, 2003.
6. C. S. Lewis, *The Problem of Pain* (New York: Macmillan, 1962), 147.

LEADER GUIDE

Today's discussion gives you the perfect opportunity to invite learners to commit their lives to Christ. Don't assume everyone in your class, even those who have attended church all their lives, have accepted Christ and are going to heaven. Take advantage of the opportunity to share how to receive Christ and urge learners to do so.

During the Session

1. State: *The Beatles asked us to imagine there's no Heaven. What if there was no Heaven?* Relate the illustration about Florence Chadwick from the study introduction on page 82. Ask: *Why do we need to see the shore and know there's a Heaven?* State that this seven-week study can help learners see the shore of Heaven through the fog. Declare: *What we will study is not wishful imagining; it's the biblical truth of a real place called Heaven.*

2. Complete the first activity of Day One (p. 83). State that the problem is most believers don't understand what awaits believers in Heaven; therefore, their image of Heaven is not always positive and they don't look forward to going there! Relate the pastor's concept of Heaven from Day One on page 84. Invite responses to the activity on page 84. Ask why some Christians have a negative concept of Heaven. Invite learners to read Revelation 13:6 and identify the three things Satan slanders. Request that they consult Isaiah 14:12-15 and state why Satan hates Heaven so much. Determine what Satan accomplishes when he convinces believers to imagine Heaven is boring. Assert that learners need to replace Satan's lies about Heaven with God's truths.☺

3. Request learners try to describe a place they've been that they would consider a small slice of paradise. State that when we try to describe something indescribable, we relate it to something people know. The Bible describes Heaven with earthly references to which we can relate. Discuss the first activity of Day Two (p. 85). Acknowledge that people cannot fully understand how wonderful a paradise is unless they visit there. But we can at least give them a good description so they want to go there themselves. That's why God revealed Heaven in earthly terms we can relate to. Read 1 Corinthians 2:9-10. Declare that God has prepared Heaven and He wants us to be excited about going there.

4. Read the first sentence (p. 87) and discuss the first activity of Day Three (p. 88). Consider why so few will make it to Heaven. Invite volunteers to read Romans 3:23 and Habakkuk 1:13. Read the title for Day Three as a

question. Ask: *If Heaven isn't our default destination, what is?* Draw on the board an intersection of two roads—a wide road going to the left and a narrow road leading to the right. State: *Imagine every person approaching a crossroad at the end of time. To the right is a narrow road leading to Heaven and life; to the left is a broad road leading to hell and destruction.* Invite someone to read aloud Revelation 20:11-15. Determine what people will encounter at the intersection of those two roads and who will be directed to the road leading to hell.

5. Consider reasons some believers don't like to talk or think about hell but why they must. Examine: *Can you fully believe in Heaven if you don't believe in hell? Why or why not? Why do we minimize Christ's work on the cross if we minimize the horrors of hell?* Discuss the second activity of Day Three (p. 89). Then request a volunteer read 2 Thessalonians 1:9. Evaluate the horror of the total absence of God. Ask: *If you were given the option between these two roads, what price would you pay to get on the narrow road?* Declare that Christ paid that price for us; we've got to decide if we'll accept His gift.

6. Request learners compare Revelation 20:15 with 21:27 and state what determines each person's road and final destination. Ask: *What determines whether your name is written in the Lamb's book of life?* Explain it's not the good deeds we've done or the bad deeds we've not done, but what we've done with God's Son. Discuss the second activity of Day Four (p. 90). Read the last paragraph of Day Four (p. 92). Urge learners if they can't answer the last question of Day Four with a positive "YES" to speak with you, a church staff member, or trusted Christian friend as soon as possible.

7. Ask the first question of Day Five (p. 92). Consider ways people on the broad road try to quench their thirst. Declare that all they receive is an unquenchable fire. Invite someone to read Jesus' invitation in Revelation 21:6 to have that thirst truly quenched. Read the Bible's final invitation in Revelation 22:17. Discuss the final activity of Day Five (p. 93). Close in prayer that learners will accept and issue Christ's invitation to enjoy Heaven with Him.❶

SCRIPTURE

"We do not want you to be uninformed, brothers, concerning those who are asleep, so that you will not grieve like the rest, who have no hope. Since we believe that Jesus died and rose again, in the same way God will bring with Him those who have fallen asleep through Jesus. For we say this to you by a revelation from the Lord: We who are still alive at the Lord's coming will certainly have no advantage over those who have fallen asleep. For the Lord Himself will descend from heaven with a shout, with the archangel's voice, and with the trumpet of God, and the dead in Christ will rise first. Then we who are still alive will be caught up together with them in the clouds to meet the Lord in the air and so we will always be with the Lord. Therefore encourage one another with these words (1 Thess. 4:13-18, HCSB).

Understanding the Present Heaven

DAY ONE

What Is the Nature of the Present Heaven?

Most of this study centers on the eternal Heaven—the place where we will live forever after the final resurrection. But because we've all had loved ones die, and we ourselves will die unless Christ returns first, we should consider what Scripture teaches about the present Heaven—the place Christians go when they die.

> **Read 1 Thessalonians 4:13-18. Why is it important to understand where Christians go when they die?** _____
> _____
> _____
> _____
> _____

When a Christian dies, he or she enters into what is referred to in theology as the intermediate state, a transitional period between our past lives on earth and our future resurrection to life on the New Earth. Usually when we refer to "Heaven," we mean the place that Christians go when they die. This is what I am calling the present or intermediate Heaven. When we tell our children "Grandma's now in Heaven," we're referring to the present Heaven.

When we die, believers in Christ will not go to the Heaven where we'll live forever. Instead, we'll go to an intermediate Heaven. In that Heaven—where those who died covered by Christ's blood are now—we'll await the time of Christ's return to the earth, our bodily resurrection, the final judgment, and the creation of the new Heavens and New Earth. If we fail to grasp this truth, we will fail to understand the biblical doctrine of Heaven.

It may seem strange to say that the Heaven we go to at death isn't eternal, yet it's true. "Christians often talk about living with God 'in Heaven' forever," writes theologian Wayne Grudem. "But in fact the biblical teaching is richer than that: it tells us that there will be new Heavens and a new earth—an entirely renewed creation—and we will live with God there. ... There will also be a new kind of unification of Heaven and earth. ... There will be a joining of Heaven and earth in this new creation."[1]

Read Matthew 24:35 and Revelation 21:1 in the margin. Underline what will happen to what we usually refer to as Heaven.

Books on Heaven often fail to distinguish between the intermediate and eternal states, using the one word—Heaven—as all-inclusive. But this has dulled our thinking and keeps us from understanding important biblical distinctions. In this study, when referring to the place believers go after death, I use terms such as *the present Heaven* or *the intermediate Heaven*. I'll refer to the eternal state as *the eternal Heaven* or *the New Earth*. I hope you can see why this is such an important distinction. The present Heaven is a temporary lodging, a waiting place until the return of Christ and our bodily resurrection. The eternal Heaven, the New Earth, is our true home, the place where we will live forever with our Lord and each other. The great redemptive promises of God will find their ultimate fulfillment on the New Earth, not in the present Heaven.

When we speak about the future New Earth, much of what we say about it may not be true of the intermediate Heaven. (For instance, we will eat and drink in our resurrection bodies on the New Earth, but that doesn't mean people eat and drink in the present Heaven.) And when we describe the present Heaven, it will not necessarily correspond with what

SCRIPTURE

"Heaven and earth will pass away, but My words will never pass away" (Matt. 24:35, HCSB).

"Then I saw a new heaven and a new earth, for the first heaven and the first earth had passed away, and the sea no longer existed" (Rev. 21:1, HCSB).

the eternal Heaven, the New Earth, will be like. Once we abandon our assumptions that Heaven cannot change, it all makes sense. God does not change; He's immutable. But God clearly says that Heaven will change. It will eventually be relocated to the New Earth (Rev. 21:1). Similarly, what we now refer to as Hell will also be relocated. After the great white throne judgment, Hell will be cast into the eternal lake of fire (Rev. 20:14-15).

How do you feel about the concept of a distinction between an intermediate and eternal Heaven?

____ I totally reject the concept.

____ It's different from everything I've ever thought about Heaven.

____ Makes perfect sense to me.

____ It's totally new to me. I'm excited about exploring the Scriptures about this.

DAY TWO

What is the Nature of the Future Heaven?

SCRIPTURE

"I saw a new heaven and a new earth .... I also saw the Holy City, new Jerusalem, coming down out of heaven from God .... Then I heard a loud voice from the throne: Look! God's dwelling is with humanity, and He will live with them. They will be His people, and God Himself will be with them and be their God" (Rev. 21:1-3, HCSB).

The present, intermediate Heaven is in the angelic realm, distinctly separate from earth. By contrast, the future Heaven will be in the human realm, on earth. Then the dwelling place of God will also be the dwelling place of humanity, in a resurrected universe.

As you read Revelation 21:1-3 in the margin, underline what John saw the new Jerusalem doing.

Heaven, God's dwelling place, will one day be on the New Earth. Notice that the new Jerusalem, which was in Heaven, will come down out of Heaven from God. Where does it go? To the New Earth. From that time on, "God's dwelling" (Rev. 21:3) will be with redeemed mankind on earth.

Some would argue that the New Earth shouldn't be called Heaven. But it seems clear to me that if God's special dwelling place is by definition Heaven, and we're told that the dwelling of God will be with mankind on earth, then Heaven and the New Earth will be essentially the same place. We're told that "the throne of God and of the Lamb" is in the new Jerusalem, which is brought down to the New Earth (Rev. 22:1). Again, it seems clear that wherever God dwells with His people and sits on His throne would be called Heaven.

That God would come down to the New Earth to live with us fits perfectly with His original plan. God could have taken Adam and Eve up to Heaven to visit with Him in His world. Instead, He came down to walk with them in their world (Gen. 3:8).

Read John 14:23 in your Bible. Fill in the blanks to state what Jesus promises to those who choose to love and obey Him:

My Father will _____ you, and we will _____ to you and _____ _____ _____ with you.

Most views of Heaven are anti-incarnational. They fail to grasp that Heaven will be God dwelling with us—resurrected people—on the resurrected earth. As Jesus is God incarnate, so the New Earth will be Heaven incarnate. Think of what Revelation 21:3 tells us—God will relocate His people and come down from Heaven to the New Earth to live with them: "God himself will be with them." Rather than our going up to live in God's home forever, God will come down to live in our home forever. Simply put, though the present Heaven is "up there," the future, eternal Heaven will be "down here." If we fail to see that distinction, we fail to understand God's plan and are unable to envision what our eternal lives will look like.

Utopian idealists who dream of mankind creating "Heaven on earth" are destined for disappointment. But though they are wrong in believing that humans can achieve a utopian existence apart from God, the reality of Heaven on earth—God dwelling with mankind in the world He made for us—will in fact be realized. It is God's dream. It is God's plan. He—not we—will accomplish it.

> Rather than our going up to live in God's home forever, God will come down to live in our home forever.

DAY THREE

What Happens When We Die?

Do We Remain Conscious After Death?

"The dust returns to the ground it came from, and the spirit returns to God who gave it" (Eccl. 12:7). At death, the human spirit goes either to Heaven or Hell. Christ depicted Lazarus and the rich man as conscious in Heaven and Hell immediately after they died (Luke 16:22-31). Jesus told the dying thief on the cross, "Today you will be with me in paradise" (Luke 23:43). The apostle Paul said that to die was to be with Christ (Phil. 1:23), and to be absent from the body was to be present with the Lord (2 Cor. 5:8). After their deaths, martyrs are pictured in Heaven, crying out to God to bring justice on earth (Rev. 6:9-11).

These passages make it clear that there is no such thing as "soul sleep," or a long period of unconsciousness between life on earth and life in Heaven. The phrase "fallen asleep" (in 1 Thess. 4:13 and similar passages) is a euphemism for death, describing the body's outward appearance. The spirit's departure from the body ends our existence on earth. The physical part of us "sleeps" until the resurrection, while the spiritual part of us relocates to a conscious existence in Heaven (Dan. 12:2-3; 2 Cor. 5:8). Some Old Testament passages (e.g., Eccl. 9:5) address outward appearances and do not reflect the fullness of New Testament revelation concerning immediate relocation and consciousness after death.

Every reference in Revelation to human beings talking and worshiping in Heaven prior to the resurrection of the dead demonstrates that our spiritual beings are conscious, not sleeping, after death.

Read Philippians 1:21-23 in your Bible. What did Paul conclude about being in this present Heaven? _____

_____

Why do you think it's "better by far" to be in the intermediate Heaven rather than this present earth? _____

SCRIPTURE

"Many of those who sleep in the dust of the earth will awake, some to eternal life, and some to shame and eternal contempt. Those who are wise will shine like the bright expanse of the heavens, and those who lead many to righteousness, like the stars forever and ever" (Dan. 12:2-3, HCSB).

_____

_____

_____

Will We Be Judged When We Die?

When we die, we face judgment, what is called the judgment of faith. The outcome of this judgment determines whether we go to the present Heaven or the present Hell. This initial judgment depends not on our works but on our faith. It is not about what we've done during our lives but about what Christ has done for us. If we have accepted Christ's atoning death for us, then when God judges us after we die, He sees His Son's sacrifice for us, not our sin. Salvation is a free gift, to which we can contribute absolutely nothing (Eph. 2:8-9; Titus 3:5).

This first judgment is not to be confused with the final judgment, or what is called the judgment of works. Both believers and unbelievers face a final judgment.

Read the passages in the margin. What does the Bible make very clear? _____

_____

_____

It's critical to understand that this judgment is a judgment of works, not of faith (1 Cor. 3:13-14). Our works do not affect our salvation, but they do affect our reward. Rewards are about our work for God, empowered by His Spirit. Rewards are conditional, dependent on our faithfulness (2 Tim. 2:12; Rev. 2:26-28; 3:21).

Unbelievers face a final judgment of works as well. The Bible tells us it will come at the great white throne, at the end of the old earth and just before the beginning of the New Earth (Rev. 20:11-13).

Opinions vary about when the judgment of works for believers will occur. Some people picture it occurring immediately after the judgment of faith, a "one at a time" judgment happening as each believer dies. Others think it happens in the present Heaven, between our death and the return of Christ. Those who believe in a pretribulational rapture often envision the judgment of works happening between the rapture and the physical return of Christ, while the tribulation is taking place on earth. Still others

SCRIPTURE

"But I tell you that men will have to give account on the day of judgment for every careless word they have spoken" (Matt. 12:36, NIV).

"For we must all appear before the tribunal of Christ, so that each may be repaid for what he has done in the body, whether good or worthless" (2 Cor. 5:10, HCSB).

believe it happens at the same time as the great white throne judgment of unbelievers, after the millennium.

DAY FOUR

Do People Have Intermediate Bodies in the Present Heaven?

Given the consistent physical descriptions of the present Heaven and those who dwell there, it seems possible—though this is certainly debatable—that between our earthly life and our bodily resurrection, God may grant us some physical form that will allow us to function as human beings while in that unnatural state "between bodies," awaiting our resurrection. Just as the intermediate state is a bridge between life on the old earth and the New Earth, perhaps intermediate bodies, or at least a physical form of some sort, serve as bridges between our present bodies and our resurrected bodies.

The martyrs in Heaven are described as wearing clothes (Rev. 6:9-11). Disembodied spirits don't wear clothes. Many consider the clothes purely symbolic of being covered in Christ's righteousness. Of course, they could also be real clothes with symbolic meaning, just as the ark of the covenant had symbolic meaning but was also a real, physical object.

Because these martyrs are also called "souls" (Rev. 6:9), some insist that they must be disembodied spirits. But the Greek word *psuche,* here translated "soul," does not normally mean disembodied spirit. On the contrary, it is typically used of a whole person, who has both body and spirit, or of animals, which are physical beings.

It appears the apostle John had a body when he visited Heaven, because he is said to have grasped, held, eaten, and tasted things there (see Rev. 10:9-10). To assume this is all figurative language is not a restriction demanded by the text but only by our presupposition that Heaven isn't a physical place.

In the apostle Paul's account of being caught up to the present Heaven (which he calls "the third Heaven"), he expresses uncertainty about whether he'd had a body there or not: "Whether in the body or apart from the body I do not know, but God knows" (2 Cor. 12:3). The fact that he thought he might have had a body in Heaven is significant. He certainly didn't dismiss the thought as impossible. His uncertainty might suggest that he sensed he had a physical form in Heaven that was body-like but somehow different from his earthly body. If he had been nothing but spirit in Heaven, it's unlikely he would say he wasn't certain whether or not he'd had a body there.

Read in your Bible Luke 16:19-31. List in the margin references to some type of body in the present Heaven and Hell.

In your opinion, do you think Jesus would have included these references if those in the present Heaven are disembodied spirits? YES   NO
Explain your response._____

_____

_____

_____

_____

If those in Heaven are granted temporary forms—and I recognize it only as a possibility—it would in no way minimize the absolute necessity or critical importance of our future bodily resurrection, which Paul emphatically establishes in 1 Corinthians 15:12-32.

We do not receive resurrection bodies immediately after death. Resurrection is not one-at-a-time. If we have intermediate forms in the intermediate Heaven, they won't be our true bodies, which have died. Continuity is only between our original and resurrection bodies. If we are given intermediate forms, they are at best temporary vessels (comparable to the human-appearing bodies that angels sometimes take on), distinct from our true bodies, which remain dead until our resurrection.

A fundamental article of the Christian faith is that the resurrected Christ now dwells in Heaven. We are told that His resurrected body on earth was physical, and that this same, physical Jesus ascended to Heaven, from which He will one day return to earth (Acts 1:11). It seems

"But Stephen, filled by the Holy Spirit, gazed into heaven. He saw God's glory, with Jesus standing at the right hand of God, and he said, 'Look! I see the heavens opened and the Son of Man standing at the right hand of God!'" (Acts 7:55-56, HCSB)

indisputable, then, to say that there is at least one physical body in the present Heaven.

Read Acts 7:55-56 in the margin. What did Stephen, the first Christian martyr, see right before he was stoned to death for his faith in Christ? _____

_____

If Christ's body in the present Heaven has physical properties, it stands to reason that others in Heaven might have physical forms as well, even if only temporary ones. If we know there is physical substance in Heaven (namely, Christ's body), can we not also assume that other references to physical objects in Heaven, including physical forms and clothing, are literal rather than figurative?

DAY FIVE

What Is Life Like in the Present Heaven?

"When he opened the fifth seal, I saw under the altar the souls of those who had been slain because of the word of God and the testimony they had maintained. They called out in a loud voice, 'How long, Sovereign Lord, holy and true, until you judge the inhabitants of the earth and avenge our blood?' Then each of them was given a white robe, and they were told to wait a little longer, until the number of their fellow servants and brothers who were to be killed as they had been was completed" (Rev. 6:9-11, NIV).

We can learn a great deal about the present Heaven from three key verses in Revelation 6:9-11.

Take a moment to carefully read that passage in the margin.

1. These people in Heaven were the same ones killed for Christ while on earth (v. 9). This demonstrates direct continuity between our identity on earth and our identity in Heaven.

2. "They called out" (v. 10) means they are able to express themselves audibly. This could suggest they exist in physical form, with vocal cords or other tangible means to express themselves.

3. People in the present Heaven can raise their voices (v. 10). This indicates that they are rational, communicative, and emotional—even passionate—beings, like people on earth.

4. Those in Heaven are free to ask God questions, which means they have an audience with God. It also means they need to learn. In Heaven, people desire understanding and pursue it.

5. People in the present Heaven know what's happening on earth (v. 10).

6. Those in Heaven see God's attributes ("Sovereign … holy and true") in a way that makes His judgment of sin more understandable.

7. Those in Heaven are distinct individuals: "Then each of them was given a white robe" (v. 11). There isn't one merged identity that obliterates uniqueness, but a distinct "each of them."

8. The martyrs' wearing white robes suggests the possibility of actual physical forms, because disembodied spirits presumably don't wear robes.

9. God answers their question (v. 11), indicating communication and process in Heaven. It also demonstrates that we won't know everything in Heaven—if we did, we would have no questions. There is learning in the present Heaven.

10. There is time in the present Heaven. The white-robed martyrs ask God a time-dependent question: "How long, Sovereign Lord … until you judge the inhabitants of the earth and avenge our blood?" (v. 10).

Unless there is some reason to believe that the realities of this passage apply only to one group of martyrs and to no one else in Heaven—and I see no such indication—then we should assume that what is true of them is also true of our loved ones already there, and will be true of us when we die.

The martyrs depicted in Revelation 6 clearly remember at least some of what happened on earth, including that they underwent great suffering. If they remember their martyrdom, there's no reason to assume they would forget other aspects of their earthly lives. In fact, we'll all likely remember much more in Heaven than we do on earth, and we will probably be able to see how God and angels intervened on our behalf when we didn't realize it.

Many books on Heaven maintain that those in Heaven cannot be aware of people and events on earth because they would be made unhappy by all the suffering and evil; thus, Heaven would not truly be Heaven.

We must keep in mind that Revelation 21:4, the verse most often quoted on the subject of sorrow in Heaven, refers specifically to the eternal Heaven, the New Earth. "He will wipe every tear from their eyes. There will be no more death or mourning or crying or pain, for the old order of things has passed away." Christ's promise of no more tears or pain comes after the end of the old earth, after the great white throne judgment, after "the old order of things has passed away" and there's no more suffering on earth.

We can be assured there will be no sorrow on the New Earth, our eternal home. But though the present Heaven is a far happier place than earth under the curse, Scripture doesn't state there can be no sorrow there. At the same time, people in Heaven are not frail beings whose joy can only be preserved by shielding them from what's really going on in the universe. Happiness in Heaven is not based on ignorance but on perspective. Those who live in the presence of Christ find great joy in worshiping God and living as righteous beings in rich fellowship in a sinless environment. And because God is continuously at work on earth, the saints watching from Heaven have a great deal to praise Him for. But those in the present Heaven are also looking forward to Christ's return, their bodily resurrection, the final judgment, and the fashioning of the New Earth from the ruins of the old.

SCRIPTURE

"Do not be amazed at this, because a time is coming when all who are in the graves will hear His voice and come out" (John 5:28-29a, HCSB).

Read Jesus' words in the margin. How will those in the present Heaven, whose physical bodies have died, know it's time for Christ's return and their bodily resurrection? _____

_____

_____

Only then and there, in our eternal home, will all evil and suffering and sorrow be washed away by the hand of God. Only then and there will we experience the fullness of joy intended by God and purchased for us by Christ at an unfathomable cost.

Meanwhile, we on this dying earth can relax and rejoice for our loved ones who are in the presence of Christ. As the apostle Paul tells us, though we naturally grieve at losing loved ones, we are not "to grieve like the rest of men, who have no hope" (1 Thess. 4:13). Our parting is not the end of our relationship, only an interruption. We have not "lost" them, because we know where they are. They are experiencing the joy of Christ's presence in a place so wonderful that Christ called it paradise. And one day, we're told, in a magnificent reunion, they and we "will be with the Lord forever. Therefore encourage each other with these words" (1 Thess. 4:17-18).

1. Wayne Grudem, *Systematic Theology: An Introduction to Biblical Doctrine* (Grand Rapids: Zondervan, 1994), 1158.

LEADER GUIDE

To the Leader
This material may be new and perhaps confusing to you and/or class participants. Encourage yourself and learners to abandon long-held assumptions about Heaven. Even if what you're learning through this week's study is different than what you or learners have always thought about heaven, that doesn't mean it's wrong or unbiblical. Allow participants to express questions or disagreements but mostly encourage them to be like the noble Bereans and examine Scripture for themselves to determine truth (Acts 17:11).

Consider following the idea in the teaching plan to use two posters to distinguish between the two Heavens. This can really help solidify these concepts in learners' minds and be a reference for later weeks of study.

Before the Session

Write "Present, Intermediate Heaven" on one large tear sheet or poster board and "Eternal Heaven, New Earth" on another.

During the Session

1. Ask: *If you asked shoppers in the mall where people go when they die, what kind of answers might you get? What answers might you get if you asked that question in church? How would you answer that question?* State that not everyone agrees on where people go after this life. Some say purgatory, soul-sleep, or nowhere. Discuss the first activity of Day One (p. 96). Even those who say believers go to Heaven might not agree on the nature of that Heaven. Randy Alcorn asserts that believers go to Heaven when they die, but not to the eternal new Heaven and earth. Display the two posters and declare that Alcorn distinguishes between a present and eternal Heaven. Invite responses to the final activity of Day One (p. 98). Encourage participants to approach God's Word with an open mind, willing to have long-held perceptions challenged or to respectfully disagree.

2. Use remarks in Day One to explain what Alcorn means by present or intermediate Heaven. Emphasize he is not referring to an intermediate state where believers float around in mindless nirvana, but an intermediate place where believers who have died wait for Christ to usher in the eternal Heaven. Discuss the second activity of Day One (p. 97). Guide participants to state the differences between the intermediate and eternal Heavens. Write responses on the two posters. (Samples: Intermediate: temporary, a waiting place, not final destination. Eternal: permanent, where God's ultimate promises are fulfilled, our true and final home.) Guide learners to identify what believers wait for in the present Heaven. (The return of Christ, our bodily resurrection, and new home in the eternal Heaven.)

3. Write "up there" on the Present Heaven poster. Invite a volunteer to read Revelation 21:1-3. Request participants state the location of the

eternal Heaven. Write "down here" on the Eternal Heaven poster. Read this statement: "Rather than our going up to live in God's home forever, God will come down to live in our home forever" (p. 99). Encourage learners to state why that is an exciting or disturbing concept to them. Declare that God made this earth for humanity. Just as He came down to be with Adam and Eve, He will come down to be with His people on the New Earth. ♫

4. Invite responses to the first activity of Day Three (p. 100). Point out that Day Three asks some very deep questions about the nature of the present Heaven. Read the italicized heading question on page 100 (Do we remain conscious after death?). Ask how participants would answer that question based on Philippians 1:21-23. Write "spirits live" on the Present Heaven poster. Invite learners to open their Bibles to 2 Corinthians 5:8 and compare that verse with Daniel 12:2-3 in the margin on page 100. Declare our bodies may sleep in the dust, but we are present with the Lord when we die. Invite someone to read 2 Corinthians 5:8-10. Ask what else this passage says about life after death. Use the remarks and activities in Day Three to distinguish between the judgment of faith and the final judgment of works. State: *Even if we're not sure when that final judgment will occur, 2 Corinthians 5:9 has some good advice to follow. What is that advice?* ♫

5. Invite participants to respond to Day Four's title question. Ask a volunteer to read the first paragraph of that day (p. 102). Write "may have intermediate bodies" on the Present Heaven poster. Use the activities and remarks in Day Four to explore the possibility of believers having some bodily form in the present Heaven. Read 1 Corinthians 15:51-52. Explain that we do not receive our new resurrected bodies until Christ takes us to our eternal Heaven. Write "resurrected bodies" on the Eternal Heaven poster. (You will explore the resurrection body more in-depth in the lesson for the week of November 6)

6. Invite someone to read Revelation 6:9-11. Guide learners to pull from these verses what life is like in the present Heaven. Ask: *Can Heaven be Heaven if you can remember what happened to you and see what's happening on earth? Explain.* Write "Jesus is there" on both posters. Consider how that truth encourages learners even if they can't fully know what the present and eternal Heavens will be like. Close in prayer.

Grasping Redemption's Far Reach

DAY ONE

Are We Just A-Passing Through?

The old gospel song, "This world is not my home, I'm just a-passing through," is a half-truth. We may pass from the earth through death, but eventually we'll be back to live on the restored earth.

God created the entire universe to be an expression of His character.

Read in your Bible Genesis 1:10,12,16-18,21,25. What did God declare about every facet of His earthly creation? _____

_____

Read Genesis 3:17. What happened to the earth because of humanity's rebellion? _____

The serpent's seduction of Adam and Eve did not catch God by surprise. He had in place a plan by which He would redeem mankind— and all of creation—from sin, corruption, and death. Just as He promises to make men and women new, He promises to renew the earth itself.

As you read the verses in the margin, circle the word "new." Then read the verses out loud, emphasizing the word "new."

SCRIPTURE

"For I will create a new heaven and a new earth" (Isa. 65:17, HCSB).

"For just as the new heavens and the new earth, which I will make, will endure before Me"—this is the LORD's declaration—"so your offspring and your name will endure" (Isa. 66:22, HCSB).

"But based on His promise, we wait for the new heavens and a new earth, where righteousness will dwell" (2 Pet. 3:13, HCSB).

"Then I saw a new heaven and a new earth, for the first heaven and the first earth had passed away, and the sea no longer existed" (Rev. 21:1, HCSB).

Many other passages allude to the new Heavens and New Earth without using those terms. God's redemptive plan climaxes not at the return of Christ, nor in the millennial kingdom, but on the New Earth. Only then will all wrongs be made right. Only then will there be no more death, crying, or pain (Rev. 21:1-4).

God's kingdom and dominion are not about what happens in some remote, unearthly place; instead, they are about what happens on the earth, which God created for His glory. God has tied His glory to the earth and everything connected with it: mankind, animals, trees, rivers, everything. "Holy, holy, holy is the Lord Almighty; the whole earth is full of his glory" (Isa. 6:3). The Hebrew here can be translated "the fullness of the earth is his glory." His glory is manifested in His creation. The earth is not disposable. It is essential to God's plan. God promises that ultimately the whole earth will be filled with His glory (Ps. 72:19; Hab. 2:14).

Read in your Bible Isaiah 11:6-10 and briefly describe an earth filled with God's glory. _____

_____

_____

_____

_____

_____

DAY TWO

Uniting Heaven and Earth

Read Ephesians 1:9-10 and fill in the blanks to complete the sentence.
God's plan of the ages is to bring _____ _____ in Heaven and on _____ together under one head, even _____.

"All things" is broad and inclusive—nothing will be left out. This verse corresponds precisely to the culmination of history that we see enacted in Revelation 21, the merging together of the once-separate realms of Heaven and earth, fully under Christ's lordship.

The hymn "This Is My Father's World" expresses this truth in its final words: "Jesus who died shall be satisfied, and earth and heaven be one."[1] Just as God and mankind are reconciled in Christ, so too the dwellings of God and mankind—Heaven and earth—will be reconciled in Christ. As God and man will be forever united in Jesus, so Heaven and earth will forever be united in the new physical universe where we will live as resurrected beings. To affirm anything less is to understate the redemptive work of Christ.

Heaven is God's home. Earth is our home. Jesus Christ, as the God-man, forever links God and mankind, and thereby forever links Heaven and earth. As Ephesians 1:10 demonstrates, this idea of earth and Heaven becoming one is explicitly biblical. Christ will make earth into Heaven and Heaven into earth. Just as the wall that separates God and mankind is torn down in Jesus, so too the wall that separates Heaven and earth will be forever demolished. There will be one universe, with all things in Heaven and on earth together under one head, Jesus Christ. "Now the dwelling of God is with men, and he will live with them" (Rev. 21:3). God will live with us on the New Earth. That will "bring all things in heaven and on earth together" (Eph. 1:10).

Read the verses in the right margin. What will God:

renew? _____

restore? _____

God's plan is that there will be no more gulf between the spiritual and physical worlds. There will be no divided loyalties or divided realms. There will be one cosmos, one universe united under one Lord—forever. This is the unstoppable plan of God. This is where history is headed.

When God walked with Adam and Eve in the garden of Eden, earth was Heaven's backyard. The New Earth will be even more than that—it will be Heaven itself. And those who know Jesus will have the privilege of living there.

SCRIPTURE

"Jesus said to them, 'I tell you the truth, at the renewal of all things, when the Son of Man sits on his glorious throne, you who have followed me will also sit on twelve thrones, judging the twelve tribes of Israel'" (Matt. 19:28, NIV).

"Heaven must welcome Him until the times of the restoration of all things, which God spoke about by the mouth of His holy prophets from the beginning" (Acts 3:21, HCSB).

DAY THREE

The Last Adam Defeats Satan

Satan successfully tempted the first Adam in Eden. The theological consequences of Adam's sin (and the redeeming work of the last Adam, Jesus Christ—the new head of the human race) are laid out in Romans 5:12-19.

Carefully read Romans 5:12-19 in your Bible. Use the chart below to contrast the first Adam and last Adam.

First Adam	Last Adam (Christ)

When Satan tempted the last Adam in the wilderness (which is what Eden's garden had become), Christ resisted him. But the Evil One was desperate to defeat Christ, to kill Him as he had the first Adam (Matt. 4:1-11; Luke 4:1-13).

Satan appeared to succeed when the last Adam died. But Jesus didn't die because He had sinned. He died because, as God's Son, He chose to pay the price for mankind's sins, tracing all the way back to the first Adam and forward to the final generation of the fallen earth. Satan's apparent victory in Christ's death was what assured the Devil's final defeat. When Christ rose from the dead, He dealt Satan a fatal blow, crushing his head, assuring both his destruction and the resurrection of mankind and the earth. Satan's grip on this world was loosened. It's still strong, but once he is cast into the lake of fire and God refashions the old earth into the New Earth, mankind and earth will slip forever from Satan's grasping hands, never again to be touched by him (Rev. 20:10).

Christ has already defeated Satan, but the full scope of His victory has not yet been manifested on earth. At Christ's ascension, God "seated him at his right hand in the heavenly realms, far above all rule and authority, power and dominion, and every title that can be given, not only in the present age but also in the one to come. And God placed all things under his feet and appointed him to be head over everything" (Eph. 1:20-22).

These words are all-inclusive, and they are past tense, not future. Christ rules the universe. And yet it is only upon Christ's physical return to the earth that Satan will be bound.

This is the "already and not yet" paradox that characterizes life on the present earth. Heaven's king is even now "ruler of the kings of the earth" (Rev. 1:5). "On his robe and on his thigh he has this name written: King of kings and Lord of lords" (Rev. 19:16).

Through Christ's redemptive work, He "disarmed the powers and authorities" and "made a public spectacle of them, triumphing over them" (Col. 2:15). His death stripped Satan of ultimate power (Heb. 2:14).

Read 1 John 3:8 in the margin. Jesus came to (choose one answer)
___ **Destroy this present earth**
___ **Destroy sinful people**
___ **Destroy the Devil's works**

SCRIPTURE

"The Son of God appeared for this purpose, to destroy the works of the devil" (1 John 3:8, NASB).

Note that it says Christ came not to destroy the world He created, but to destroy the works of the Devil, which were to twist and pervert and ruin what God had made. Redemption will forever destroy the Devil's work by removing its hold on creation, and reversing its consequences. It is Satan's desire to destroy the world. God's intent is not to destroy the world but to deliver it from destruction. His plan is to redeem this fallen world, which He designed for greatness.

Redeemed mankind will reign with Christ over the earth. The gates of Satan's false kingdom will not prevail against Christ's church (Matt. 16:18).

The outcome of the great war is not in question. It is certain. Christ will reign victoriously forever. The only question we must answer is this: Will we fight on His side or against Him? We answer this question not just once, with our words, but daily, with our choices.

DAY FOUR

Removing the Curse

What amazing declaration about Heaven is made in the first sentence of Revelation 22:3? Write it in the margin and then say it out loud a few times.

If the Bible said nothing else about life in the eternal Heaven, the New Earth, these words would tell us a vast amount. No more curse.

What would our lives be like if the curse were lifted? One day we will know firsthand—but even now there's much to anticipate.

After Adam sinned, God said, "Cursed is the ground [earth] because of you" (Gen. 3:17). When the curse is reversed, we will no longer engage in "painful toil" (v. 17) but will enjoy satisfying caretaking. No longer will the earth yield "thorns and thistles" (v. 18), defying our dominion and repaying us for corrupting it. No longer will we "return to the ground [from which we] were taken" (v. 19), swallowed up in death as unrighteous stewards who ruined ourselves and the earth.

Our welfare is inseparable from earth's welfare. Our destiny is inseparable from earth's destiny. That's why the curse on mankind required that the earth be cursed and why the earth will also be resurrected when we are resurrected. The curse will be reversed.

As a result of the curse, the first Adam could no longer eat from the tree of life, which presumably would have made him live forever in his sinful state (Gen. 3:22). Death, though a curse in itself, was also the only way out from under the curse—and that is only because God had come up with a way to defeat death and restore mankind's relationship with Him.

Christ came to remove the curse of sin and death (Rom. 8:2). He is the second Adam, who will undo the damage wrought by the first Adam (1 Cor. 15:22,45; Rom. 5:15-19). In the cross and the resurrection, God made a way not only to restore His original design for mankind but also to expand it. In our resurrection bodies, we will again dwell on earth—a New

Earth—completely free of the curse. Unencumbered by sin, human activity will lead naturally to a prosperous and magnificent culture.

Under the curse, human culture has not been eliminated, but it has been severely hampered by sin, death, and decay. Before the fall, food was readily available with minimal labor. Time was available to pursue thoughtful aesthetic ideas, to work for the sheer pleasure of it, to please and glorify God by developing skills and abilities. Since the fall, generations have lived and died after spending most of their productive years eking out an existence in the pursuit of food, shelter, and protection against theft and war. Mankind has been distracted and debilitated by sickness and sin. Our cultural development has likewise been stunted and twisted, and sometimes misdirected—though not always. Even though our depravity means we have no virtue that makes us worthy of our standing before God, we are nevertheless "made in God's likeness" (Jas. 3:9). Consequently, some things we do, even in our fallenness, such as painting, building, performing beautiful music, finding cures for diseases, and other cultural, scientific, commercial, and aesthetic pursuits, are good.

The removal of the curse means that people, culture, and the earth will again be as God intended. The lifting of the curse comes at a terrible price: "Christ redeemed us from the curse of the law by becoming a curse for us—for it is written: 'Cursed is everyone who is hanged on a tree'" (Gal. 3:13, esv). God's law shows us how far short we fall. But Jesus took on Himself the curse of sin, satisfying God's wrath. By taking the curse upon Himself and defeating it through His resurrection, Jesus guaranteed the lifting of the curse from mankind and from the earth.

The removal of the curse will be as thorough and sweeping as the redemptive work of Christ. In bringing us salvation, Christ has already undone some of the damage in our hearts, but in the end He will finally and completely restore His entire creation to what God originally intended.

Read Romans 8:20-22 in margin. Circle the words that describe the present created world. Underline the adjectives that will describe this created earth when Jesus lifts the curse once and for all.

Christ will turn back the curse and restore to humanity all that we lost in Eden, and He will give us much more besides.

SCRIPTURE

"Christ redeemed us from the curse of the law by becoming a curse for us—for it is written, 'Cursed is everyone who is hanged on a tree'" (Gal 3:13, ESV).

SCRIPTURE

"For the creation was subjected to futility— not willingly, but because of Him who subjected it—in the hope that the creation itself will also be set free from the bondage of corruption into the glorious freedom of God's children. For we know that the whole creation has been groaning together with labor pains until now" (Rom. 8:20-22, HCSB).

DAY FIVE

How Far Does Christ's Redemptive Work Extend?

Jesus came not only to save spirits from damnation. That would have been, at most, a partial victory. No, He came to save His whole creation from death. That means our bodies too, not just our spirits. It means the earth, not just humanity. And it means the universe, not just the earth. Christ's victory over the curse will not be partial. Death will not just limp away wounded. It will be annihilated, utterly destroyed:

As you read Isaiah 25:7-8 in the margin, circle the actions God will take.

Isaac Watts's magnificent hymn "Joy to the World" is theologically on target:

No more let sins and sorrows grow
Nor thorns infest the ground;
He comes to make His blessings flow
Far as the curse is found.

God will lift the curse, not only morally (in terms of sins) and psycho-logically (in terms of sorrows), but also physically (in terms of thorns in the ground). How far does Christ's redemptive work extend? *Far as the curse is found.* If redemption failed to reach the farthest boundaries of the curse, it would be incomplete. The God who rules the world with truth and grace won't be satisfied until every sin, every sorrow, every thorn is reckoned with.

Jesus came not only to rescue people from ultimate destruction. He came also to rescue the entire universe from ultimate destruction. He will transform our dying earth into a vital New Earth, fresh and uncontami-nated, no longer subject to death and destruction.

The curse is real, but it is *temporary.* Jesus is the cure for the curse. He came to set derailed human history back on its tracks. Earth won't be

SCRIPTURE

"He will destroy death forever. The Lord GOD will wipe away the tears from every face and remove His people's disgrace from the whole earth, for the LORD has spoken" (Isa. 25:8, HCSB).

put out of its misery; it will be infused with a greater life than it has ever known, at last becoming all that God meant for it to be.

We have never seen the earth as God made it. Our planet as we know it is a shadowy, halftone image of the original. But it does whet our appetites for the New Earth, doesn't it? If the present earth, so diminished by the curse, is at times so beautiful and wonderful; if our bodies, so diminished by the curse, are at times overcome with a sense of the earth's beauty and wonder; then how magnificent will the New Earth be? And what will it be like to experience the New Earth in something else we've never known: perfect bodies?

What place on earth would you like to see and experience but are unable because of financial and/or physical limitations?_____

_____

Do you think you'll be able to see and experience this place when you are in God's eternal Heaven? Explain._____

_____

_____

_____

A mature Christian Bible student wrote me a note after reading a draft of this book: "I realize now that I have always thought that when we die we go immediately to our eternal home. After I was there, that would be the end of the story. I wouldn't care about what happened to earth and everything on it. Why *should* I care about a doomed planet?"

Without Christ, both the earth and mankind would be doomed. But Christ came, died, and rose from the grave. He brought deliverance, not destruction. Because of Christ, we are not doomed, and neither is the earth.

Earth cannot be delivered from the curse by being destroyed. It can only be delivered by being *resurrected*. As we'll see next week, Christ's resurrection is the forerunner of our own, and our resurrection is the forerunner of the earth's.

Use 2 Peter 3:13 to begin talking with God and then continue with your own thoughts: "Lord, in keeping with Your promise, I am so looking forward to a new heaven and a new earth because ..."

SCRIPTURE

"But based on His promise, we wait for the new heavens and a new earth, where righteousness will dwell" (2 Pet. 3:13, HCSB).

1. Maltbie D. Babcock, "This Is My Father's World," 1901.

To the Leader

This teaching plan makes use of several songs. You might not be completely comfortable obtaining and using those songs, but keep in mind some adults in your class may learn best through music. Your extra efforts and a step outside your comfort zone could make all the difference for them.

Before the Session

1. Obtain the lyrics to "This World Is Not My Home" (can be easily found with an Internet search).

2. Provide copies of "This Is My Father's World" (*The Baptist Hymnal*, No. 46, 2008 edition; No. 43, 1991 edition) and "Joy to the World" (No. 181, 2008; No. 87, 1991).

During the Session

1. Read the first few lines of the gospel song "This World Is Not My Home." Ask if participants agree with the songwriter's sentiments and why. Invite someone to read the first paragraph of Day One (p. 109). Ask: *How do you feel about coming back to live on this earth? Why?* Declare that this week's study challenges adults to grasp that Christ's redemptive work on the cross reaches far enough to redeem this physical earth.

2. Discuss the first question of Day One (p. 109). God created earth to be an expression of His character. Many songwriters, including psalmists, have created songs to try to express God's character in nature. Distribute hymnals and ask learners to turn to "This Is My Father's World" (place a marker there, they'll return to it in Step 3) and state from the first two verses how God's character is evident in the natural world. Read the first two lines of the third verse. Note the hymn writer recognized there is wrong in this world, then analyze how it got into God's perfect creation. Discuss the second bolded question (using Gal. 3:13) in Day One (p. 109). Declare that this present world is under a curse. Ask: *From what you know about God, will He leave something He created good under a curse? Explain.* Declare that God promises to renew the earth. Follow the instructions for the bolded activity at the end of Day One (p. 110).❤

3. Invite someone to read the last two lines of the third verse of "This Is My Father's World." Ask: *Why do you think it will satisfy Jesus for earth and Heaven to be one?* (Consult the first activity of Day Two, p. 110.)

Explain that "bring together" means to sum up and gather all the pieces into a whole. Declare that God is going to gather all the pieces of His creation that have been shattered by sin and unite them under Christ's lordship. Invite participants to imagine they have created a perfect masterpiece. Ask: *If that masterpiece was damaged, would you destroy or restore it? Why?* Encourage participants to list words that begin with the prefix "re." (Examples: reconcile, redeem, restore, recover, return, renew, resurrect, reclaim) Explain that "re" suggests a return to an original condition. Discuss the second activity of Day Two (p. 111). Read Psalm 24:1-2. Declare that because the earth is God's perfect masterpiece, He is going to redeem, restore, renew, and reclaim it.

4. Point out that redemption was prophesied before God even pronounced the curse on the earth. Ask someone to read Genesis 3:15. Declare that the first Adam's sin brought the curse but the second Adam's death and resurrection broke the curse. Request participants state from Day Three what Christ assured when He crushed Satan's head. Discuss the last activity of Day Three (p. 113). Evaluate the difference between destroying the earth and destroying the Devil's works.

5. Complete the first activity of Day Four (p. 114) as an entire class. Ask: *What would our lives be like if the curse were lifted?* Use remarks in Day Four to aid the discussion. Ask: *A song declares God has the whole world in His hands; do you believe that? Why? What happened to those hands so He could redeem earth? How did Christ reverse the curse on this earth and its inhabitants?* (See Gal. 3:13 in Day Four.) Discuss the last activity of Day Four (p. 115).

6. Ask participants to turn to "Joy to the World" in the hymnal. Explain that Isaac Watts did not write this as a Christmas carol but a paraphrase of Psalm 98, where the created world rejoices when the Lord returns to rule the earth. Urge participants to scan the verses and answer: *What will rejoice when Christ returns? Why will the earth itself rejoice? How far will Christ's redemptive work reach? What does "as far as the curse is found" mean to you?* Explain what God will do morally, psychologically, and physically when the curse is ultimately removed. Ask: *How does this present earth whet your appetite for the New Earth?* Invite responses to the questions in the second activity of Day Five (p. 117). Close in prayer.

Anticipating Resurrection

DAY ONE

Why Is Resurrection So Important?

In the late 1990s, a group of scholars assembled to evaluate whether Jesus actually said the things attributed to Him by the Gospel writers. Although they employed remarkably subjective criteria in their evaluation of Scripture, members of the self-appointed "Jesus Seminar" were widely quoted by the media as authorities on the Christian faith.

Marcus Borg, a Jesus Seminar leader, said this of Christ's resurrection: "As a child, I took it for granted that Easter meant that Jesus literally rose from the dead. I now see Easter very differently. For me, it is irrelevant whether or not the tomb was empty. Whether Easter involved something remarkable happening to the physical body of Jesus is irrelevant."[1]

What Borg calls irrelevant—the physical resurrection of Christ's body— the apostle Paul considered absolutely essential to the Christian faith.

Read 1 Corinthians 15:14-19 in your Bible. List in the margin everything that would be true if Christ had not physically risen from the dead.

The physical resurrection of Jesus Christ is the cornerstone of redemption—both for mankind and for the earth. Indeed, without Christ's resurrection and what it means—an eternal future for fully restored human beings dwelling on a fully restored earth—there is no Christianity.

The Resurrection is Physical. Christians tend to spiritualize the resurrection of the dead. (For Paul's exposition of the resurrection of the dead, see 1 Cor. 15:12-58.) They don't reject it as a doctrine, but they deny its essential meaning: a permanent return to a physical existence in a physical universe.

Vital truth #1: The resurrection is physical.

Of Americans who believe in a resurrection of the dead, two-thirds believe they will not have bodies after the resurrection.[2] But this is self-contradictory. A non-physical resurrection is like a sunless sunrise. There's no such thing. Resurrection means that we will have bodies. If we didn't have bodies, we wouldn't be resurrected!

Genesis 2:7 says, "The Lord God formed the man from the dust of the ground and breathed into his nostrils the breath of life, and the man became a living being." The Hebrew word for "living being" is *nephesh,* often translated "soul." The point at which Adam became *nephesh* is when God joined his body (dust) and spirit (breath) together. Adam was not a living human being until he had both material (physical) and immaterial (spiritual) components. Thus, the essence of humanity is not just spirit, but spirit joined with body. Your body does not merely house the real you—it is as much a part of who you are as your spirit is.

When God sent Jesus to die, it was for our bodies as well as our spirits. He came to redeem not just "the breath of life" (spirit) but also "the dust of the ground" (body). When we die, it isn't that our real self goes to the present Heaven and our fake self goes to the grave; it's that part of us goes to the present Heaven and part goes to the grave to await our bodily resurrection. We will never be all that God intended for us to be until body and spirit are again joined in resurrection. (If we do have physical forms in the intermediate state, clearly they will not be our original or ultimate bodies.)

Continuity Is Critical. "Therefore, if anyone is in Christ, he is a new creation; the old has gone, the new has come!" (2 Cor. 5:17). Becoming a new creation sounds as if it involves a radical change, and indeed it does. But though we become new people when we come to Christ, we still remain the same people.

Vital truth #2: Continuity is critical.

Conversion does not mean eliminating the old but transforming it. Despite the radical changes that occur through salvation, death, and resurrection, we remain who we are. We have the same history, appearance, memory, interests, and skills. This is the principle of *redemptive continuity.*

God will not scrap His original creation and start over. Instead, He will take His fallen, corrupted children and restore, refresh, and renew us to our original design.

As you read Psalm 139:13-14 in the margin underline words that describe your original design.

Likewise, the New Earth will still be earth, but a changed earth. It will be converted and resurrected, but it will still be earth and recognizable as such. Just as those reborn through salvation maintain continuity with the people they were, so too the world will be reborn in continuity with the old world (Matt. 19:28).

If we don't grasp redemptive continuity, we cannot understand the nature of our resurrection. Continuity is evident in passages that discuss resurrection, including 1 Corinthians 15:53 (see margin). It is *this* (the perishable and mortal) which puts on *that* (the imperishable and immortal). Likewise, it is *we*, the very same people who walk this earth, who will walk the New Earth. "And so *we* will be with the Lord forever" (1 Thess. 4:17, emphasis added).

DAY TWO

The Nature of Our New Bodies: Christ's Resurrected Life Is the Model for Ours

The empty tomb is the ultimate proof that Christ's resurrection body was the same body that died on the cross. If resurrection meant the creation of a new body, Christ's original body would have remained in the tomb. When Jesus said to His disciples after His resurrection, "It is I myself," He was emphasizing to them that He was the same person—in spirit *and* body—who had gone to the cross (Luke 24:39).

Read John 20:24-29 in your Bible. What was visible, tangible evidence that Jesus' resurrected body was the same body that died on the cross? _____

_____

_____

This is the most basic truth about our resurrected bodies: They are the same bodies God created for us, but they will be raised to greater perfection than we've ever known. We don't know everything about them, of course, but we do know a great deal. Scripture does not leave us in the dark about our resurrection bodies.

Because we each have a physical body, we already have the single best reference point for envisioning a new body. It's like the new upgrade of my word processing software. When I heard there was an upgrade available, I didn't say, "I have no idea what it will be like." I knew that for the most part it would be like the old program, only better. Sure, it has some new features that I didn't expect, and I'm glad for them. But I certainly recognize it as the same program I've used for a decade.

Likewise, when we receive our resurrected bodies, we'll no doubt have some welcome surprises—maybe even some new features (though no glitches or programming errors)—but we'll certainly recognize our new bodies as being ours. God has given us working models to guide our imagination about what our new bodies will be like on the New Earth.

Not only do we know what our present bodies are like, we also have an example in Scripture of what a resurrection body is like. We're told a great deal about Christ's resurrected body.

Read 1 John 3:2 in the margin. Why will studying Christ's resurrected body in Scripture help us understand what our own resurrected bodies will be like? _____

_____

_____

_____

Strangely, though Jesus in His resurrected body proclaimed, "I am not a ghost" (Luke 24:39, nlt), countless Christians think they will be ghosts in the eternal Heaven. They think they'll be disembodied spirits.

SCRIPTURE

"Dear friends, we are God's children now, and what we will be has not yet been revealed. We know that when He appears, we will be like Him because we will see Him as He is" (1 John 3:2, HCSB).

Jesus walked the earth in His resurrection body for 40 days, showing us how we would live as resurrected human beings. The risen Jesus walked and talked with two disciples on the Emmaus road (Luke 24:13-35). They asked Him questions; He taught them and guided them in their understanding of Scripture. They saw nothing different enough about Him to tip them off to His identity until "their eyes were opened" (v. 31). They saw the resurrected Jesus as a normal, everyday human being.

The times Jesus spent with His disciples after His resurrection were remarkably normal (John 21:4-5,12). On one occasion, however, Christ suddenly appeared in the room where the disciples were gathered (John 20:19). Christ's body could be touched and clung to and could consume food, yet it could apparently "materialize" as well. How is this possible? Could it be that a resurrection body is structured in such a way as to allow its molecules to pass through solid materials or to suddenly become visible or invisible? Though we know that Christ could do these things, we're not explicitly told we'll be able to. It may be that some aspects of His resurrection body are unique because of His divine nature.

By observing the resurrected Christ, we learn not only about resurrected bodies but also about resurrected relationships. Christ communicated with His disciples and showed His love to them as a group and as individuals. He instructed them and entrusted a task to them (Acts 1:4-8). The fact that Jesus picked up His relationships where they'd left off is a foretaste of our own lives after we are resurrected. We will experience continuity between our current lives and our resurrected lives, with the same memories and relational histories.

Once we understand that Christ's resurrection is the prototype for the resurrection of mankind and the earth, we realize that Scripture has given us an interpretive precedent for approaching passages concerning human resurrection and life on the New Earth. Shouldn't we interpret passages alluding to resurrected people living on the New Earth as literally as those concerning Christ's resurrected life during the 40 days He walked on the old earth?

Read 1 Corinthians 15:20-23 in your Bible. Write your thoughts about what it means for Christ to be the "firstfruits" of all who will be raised. _____

_____

_____

_____

_____

_____

DAY THREE

The Nature of Our New Bodies: Glorious

We've established that Christ's resurrected body, before His ascension, was quite normal in appearance. But what is Christ's "glorious body" like (see Phil. 3:20-21)? We are given a picture on the mount of transfiguration (Matt. 17:2). The transfiguration appears to have given us a preview of Christ's glorified body. In Revelation 1:12-18, John describes the glorified Christ he saw in the present Heaven.

Read Revelation 1:12-18 in your Bible. Describe how John saw the glorified Christ. _____

_____

_____

In comparison to both Matthew 17 and Revelation 1, it appears that the risen Christ, before His ascension, was not yet fully glorified. If He would have been glorified, surely His identity would have been immediately apparent to Mary Magdalene (John 20:14), the disciples on the Emmaus road (Luke 24:15-16), and Peter and the apostles when they saw Him on the shore (John 21:4).

Read Paul's report of encountering the glorified Christ in Acts 22:6-11. What is similar to the accounts in Matthew and Revelation?_____

_____

_____

SCRIPTURE

"But our citizenship is in heaven, from which we also eagerly wait for a Savior, the Lord Jesus Christ. He will transform the body of our humble condition into the likeness of His glorious body, by the power that enables Him to subject everything to Himself" (Phil. 3:20-21, HCSB).

"He was transformed in front of them, and His face shone like the sun. Even His clothes became as white as the light" (Matt. 17:2, HCSB).

It appears that Paul's unredeemed eyes were not yet ready to behold the glorified Christ.

Certainly, the glorified Christ will be by far the most glorious Being in Heaven. Yet, as we will see, Scripture indicates that we too, in a secondary and derivative way, will reflect God's glory in physical brightness.

Scripture speaks of the likeness of Adam and the likeness of Christ, making some distinction between them: "And just as we have borne the likeness of the earthly man, so shall we bear the likeness of the man from heaven" (1 Cor. 15:49). Christ will remain a man, but His deity that was once veiled in His humanity will shine through it. Because of the fall and the curse, we have never been or seen human beings who are fully functional as God's image-bearers, conveying the brightness and majesty of His being. But that day is coming. Christ, the God-man, the new Head of our human race, will be the ultimate Image-bearer, fully conveying the brightness and majesty of the Almighty.

Note, however, that the difference between Adam and Christ, which Paul speaks of in 1 Corinthians 15:45-49, is not that one was a physical being and the other wasn't. It was that Adam was under sin and the curse, and Christ was untouched by sin and the curse. Jesus was and is a human being, "in every respect like us" (Heb. 2:17, nlt), except with respect to sin. So although we should recognize that our resurrection bodies will be glorious in ways that our current bodies are not, we should also realize that those bodies will continue to be—in both the same and in greater ways—the functional physical bodies that God designed for us from the beginning.

DAY FOUR

The Nature of Our New Bodies: Imperishable

Read 1 Corinthians 15:42-44. Use the chart at the top of the next page to summarize the contrasts between our earthly bodies and our resurrection bodies.

EARTHLY BODY	**RESURRECTION BODY**
Sown in _____	Raised in _____
Sown in _____	Raised in _____
Sown in _____	Raised in _____
Sown a _____ body	Raised a _____ body

When Paul uses the term "spiritual body" (1 Cor. 15:44), he is not talking about a body made of spirit, or an incorporeal body—there is no such thing. *Body* means corporeal: flesh and bones. The word *spiritual* here is an adjective describing *body*, not negating its meaning. A spiritual body is first and foremost a real body or it would not qualify to be called a body. Paul could have simply said, "It is sown a natural body, it is raised a spirit," if that were the case. Judging from Christ's resurrection body, a spiritual body appears most of the time to look and act like a regular physical body, with the exception that it may have (and in Christ's case it does have) some powers of a metaphysical nature; that is, beyond normal physical abilities.

Paul goes on to say, "And just as we have borne the likeness of the earthly man, so shall we bear the likeness of the man from heaven. I declare to you, brothers, that flesh and blood cannot inherit the kingdom of God, nor does the perishable inherit the imperishable. ... We will be changed. For the perishable must clothe itself with the imperishable, and the mortal with immortality. When the perishable has been clothed with the imperishable, and the mortal with immortality, then the saying that is written will come true: 'Death has been swallowed up in victory.' 'Where, O death, is your victory? Where, O death, is your sting?'" (1 Cor. 15:49-50,52-55).

When Paul says that "flesh and blood cannot inherit the kingdom of God," he's referring to our flesh and blood *as they are now:* cursed and under sin. Our present bodies are fallen and destructible, but our future bodies—though still bodies in the fullest sense—will be untouched by sin and indestructible. They will be like Christ's resurrection body—both physical *and* indestructible.

A body need not be destructible in order to be real. Our destructibility is an aberration of God's created norm. Death, disease, and the deterioration of age are products of sin. Because there was no death before the fall, presumably Adam and Eve's original bodies were either indestructible or self-repairing (perhaps healed by the tree of life, as suggested in Revelation 22:2). Yet they were truly flesh and blood.

Scripture portrays resurrection as involving both fundamental continuity and significant dissimilarity. We dare not minimize the dissimilarities—for our glorification will certainly involve a dramatic and marvelous transformation. But, in my experience, the great majority of Christians have underemphasized continuity. They end up thinking of our transformed selves as no longer being ourselves, and the transformed earth as no longer being the earth. In some cases, they view the glorified Christ as no longer being the same Jesus who walked the earth—a belief that early Christians recognized as heresy.

Many of us look forward to Heaven more now than we did when our bodies functioned well. Joni Eareckson Tada says it well: "Somewhere in my broken, paralyzed body is the seed of what I shall become. The paralysis makes what I am to become all the more grand when you contrast atrophied, useless legs against splendorous resurrected legs. I'm convinced that if there are mirrors in heaven (and why not?), the image I'll see will be unmistakably 'Joni,' although a much better, brighter Joni."[3]

Inside your body, even if it is failing, is the blueprint for your resurrection body. You may not be satisfied with your current body or mind—but you'll be thrilled with your resurrection upgrades. With them you'll be better able to serve and glorify God and enjoy an eternity of wonders He has prepared for you.

What do you look forward to doing with your glorious, resurrected body in Heaven? _____

_____

_____

_____

_____

_____

_____

_____

_____

Scripture portrays resurrection as involving both fundamental continuity and significant dissimilarity.

DAY FIVE

Why Does All Creation Await Our Resurrection?

The gospel is far greater than most of us imagine. It isn't just good news for us—it's good news for animals, plants, stars, and planets. It's good news for the sky above and the earth below. Albert Wolters says, "The redemption in Jesus Christ means the restoration of an original good creation."[4]

Many of us have come to think of redemption far too narrowly. That's why we're fooled into thinking that Heaven must be fundamentally different from earth—because in our minds, earth is bad, irredeemable, beyond hope. But let's not forget that God called the original earth "very good"— the true earth, as He designed it to be (Gen. 1:31).

The breadth and depth of Christ's redemptive work will escape us as long as we think it is limited to humanity.

As you read God's plan for the church in Colossians 1:16-20 in the margin, underline what Christ reigns over, cares about, and will restore and renew.

God was pleased to reconcile to himself *all things, on earth and in Heaven.* The Greek words for "all things," *ta panta,* are extremely broad in their scope.[5]

The power of Christ's resurrection is enough not only to remake us, but also to remake every inch of the universe—mountains, rivers, plants, animals, stars, nebulae, quasars, and galaxies. Christ's redemptive work extends resurrection to the far reaches of the universe. This is a stunning affirmation of God's greatness. It should move our hearts to wonder and praise.

Do you ever sense creation's restlessness? Do you hear groaning in the cold night wind? Do you feel the forest's loneliness, the ocean's agitation? Do you hear longing in the cries of whales? Do you see blood and pain in the eyes of wild animals, or the mixture of pleasure and pain in the eyes of your

SCRIPTURE

"For by him all things were created: things in heaven and on earth, visible and invisible, whether thrones or powers or rulers or authorities; all things were created by him and for him. He is before all things, and in him all things hold together. And he is the head of the body, the church; he is the beginning and the firstborn from among the dead, so that in everything he might have the supremacy. For God was pleased to have all his fullness dwell in him, and through him to reconcile to himself all things, whether things on earth or things in heaven, by making peace through his blood, shed on the cross" (Col. 1:16-20, NIV).

pets? Despite vestiges of beauty and joy, something on this earth is terribly wrong. Not only God's creatures but even inanimate objects seem to feel it. But there's also hope, visible in springtime after a hard winter. As Martin Luther put it, "Our Lord has written the promise of the resurrection not in books alone, but in every leaf in springtime."[6] The creation hopes for, even anticipates, *resurrection*. That's exactly what Scripture tells us:

> "The creation waits in eager expectation for the sons of God to be revealed. For the creation was subjected to frustration, not by its own choice, but by the will of the one who subjected it, in hope that the creation itself will be liberated from its bondage to decay and brought into the glorious freedom of the children of God.
>
> We know that the whole creation has been groaning as in the pains of childbirth right up to the present time. Not only so, but we ourselves, who have the firstfruits of the Spirit, groan inwardly as we wait eagerly for our adoption as sons, the redemption of our bodies" (Rom. 8:19-23).

Last week you examined in Romans 8:20-22 a frustrated groaning creation. Now that you've read "the rest of the story," state what else the created world is doing. _____

_____
_____
_____
_____
_____

Our adoption will be finalized and our bodies redeemed. We will be fully human, with righteous spirits and incorruptible bodies.

What does it mean that creation waits for God's children to be revealed? Our Creator, the Master Artist, will put us on display to a wide-eyed universe. Our revelation will be an unveiling, and we will be seen as what we are, as what we were intended to be—God's image-bearers. We will glorify Him by ruling over the physical universe with creativity and camaraderie, showing respect and benevolence for all we rule. Our adoption will be finalized and our bodies redeemed. We will be fully human, with righteous spirits and incorruptible bodies.

Jesus Christ died to secure for us a resurrected life on a resurrected earth. Let's be careful to speak of it in terms that deliver us from our misconceptions and do justice to the greatness of Christ's redemptive work.

1. Marcus J. Borg and N. T. Wright, *The Meaning of Jesus: Two Visions* (San Francisco: HarperSanFrancisco, 1998), 129-31.
2. *Time* (March 24, 1997), 75, quoted in Paul Marshall with Lela Gilbert, *Heaven Is Not My Home: Learning to Live in God's Creation* (Nashville: Word, 1998), 234.
3. Joni Eareckson Tada, *Heaven: Your Real Home* (Grand Rapids: Zondervan, 1995), 39.
4 Albert M. Wolters, *Creation Regained: Biblical Basics for a Reformational Worldview* (Grand Rapids: Eerdmans, 1985), 11.
5. Ibid., 59.
6. Frank S. Mead, ed., *Encyclopedia of Religious Quotations* (London: Peter Davies, 1965), 379.

LEADER GUIDE

To the Leader
It would be beneficial to read the study notes and word studies for 1 Corinthians 15:12-58 on *mystudybible.com*. As participants discuss the Day 2 activity related to 1 Corinthians 15:20-23 it may be helpful for you to explain: "Firstfruits refers to the guarantee that Christ's resurrection is the first-of-a-kind resurrection that promises others will follow in the end time. ... Since Christ was the first to arise from the dead, His resurrection is the basis for the resurrection of all believers." (*mystudybible.com*)

During the Session

1. Request that participants identify absolute essentials for camping, skiing, and beach trips. (Option: Complete this exercise in teams. Adjust the activities to fit your class.) Ask: *What are absolute essentials of the Christian faith?* Invite someone to read the statement by Marcus Borg in Day One (p. 120). Ask: *Is Christ's resurrection essential or irrelevant? Why?* Complete the first activity (p. 120).

2. Assert that Christ has been resurrected and believers will be too. Alcorn points out in Day One two vital truths we must recognize about our resurrection. (The resurrection is physical and continuity is critical.) Ask: *Why would Alcorn say a non-physical resurrection is like a sunless sunrise?* The question to resolve is whether God cares about just the soul or the body as well. Ask: *Which part of us—the dust of the ground or the breath of life—did Christ die to redeem?* Request that learners state the most common emotions associated with physical death. Ask someone to read Ecclesiastes 3:11. Declare that death seems unnatural to us because it is; God designed us to live eternally in physical bodies on a physical earth. That's accomplished with a physical resurrection.☊

3. Ask a volunteer to identify the second vital truth on page 121 (continuity is critical). Inquire: *In other words, we stay the same people when we are resurrected. Does that sound like a contradiction to 2 Corinthians 5:17? Explain.* Lead participants to evaluate how they can be transformed, yet still the same. Explain the principle of redemptive continuity. Examine how redemptive continuity is evident in 1 Corinthians 15:53. Ask: *Are you comforted or disappointed to hear you'll remain you? Why?* Discuss the Psalm 139 activity on page 122.

4. Acknowledge that we'd like to know what our resurrected bodies will be like. We can see clues in Christ's resurrected body. First we must recognize Christ's resurrected body was the same body that died on the cross. Discuss the two activities on page 123. State that we get ideas about the nature of our resurrected bodies from our present bodies and from Christ's resurrected body in Scripture. Guide the class to evaluate from

Luke 24:36-43 what their own resurrected bodies will be like. Point out it is unclear if our resurrected bodies can "materialize" as Jesus' did. Mostly, Jesus engaged in normal human activities in His resurrected body. Examine John 21:1-14. Discuss: *What can we discern about our own resurrected relationships from Jesus' relationships?* Ask someone to read the final paragraph of Day Two (p. 124). Invite responses to those questions and the final activity (p. 124). Summarize the first thing we learn about the nature of our resurrected bodies is that Christ's resurrected body is a prototype. Use the analogy of a software upgrade to explain how it will be the same body but much better.☊

5. Declare that our resurrected bodies will be glorious. Again we look to Christ for clues. Explain that three of the disciples were given a preview of Christ's glorious body at the transfiguration. Invite someone to read Matthew 17:2. Ask: *If you had been one of those disciples, what general impression would you have gained?* Invite responses to the first two bolded activities in Day 3 (p. 125). Ask: *Since Christ's resurrected body is the prototype, what can we know about our resurrected bodies?* (We will be God's image-bearer and reflect His glory with physical brightness.) Consider how 1 Corinthians 15:49 supports that truth.

6. Encourage participants to state from Day Four's title another exciting truth about the nature of the resurrected body. Explain that Paul used the metaphor of a seed being planted and then coming to life as something new and better to illustrate the physical body being buried and raised to something glorious. Read 1 Corinthians 15:35-38. Explain that our bodies will be different but recognizable as coming from that seed. Use the chart on page 127 to analyze 1 Corinthians 15:42-44. Read 1 Corinthians 15:45-55. State that Scripture affirms both fundamental continuity (we will be the same) and significant dissimilarity (we will be transformed). Read the final paragraph of Day Four (p. 128) and invite responses to the bolded activity.

7. State that we're not the only ones looking forward to our physical resurrection—all creation is. Discuss the second activity of Day Five (p. 130). Ask: *Why does creation groan? Why is it eager for humanity to be resurrected?* Read the quote in the margin of page 130. Close with a prayer of praise.

Seeing the Earth Restored

DAY ONE

Where and When Will Our Deliverance Come?

If God were to end history and reign forever in a distant Heaven, earth would be remembered as a graveyard of sin and failure. Instead, earth will be redeemed and resurrected. In the end it will be a far greater world, even for having gone through the birth pains of suffering and sin—yes, even sin. The New Earth will justify the old earth's disaster, make good out of it, putting it in perspective. It will preserve and perpetuate earth's original design and heritage.

Isaiah and the prophets make clear the destiny of God's people. They will live in peace and prosperity, as free people in their promised land.

Read the passages from Isaiah below. Record one or two promises that particularly appeal to you.

Isaiah 60:1-22 _____

_____

_____

Isaiah 65:17-25 _____

_____

_____

SCRIPTURE

"All these people were still living by faith when they died. They did not receive the things promised; they only saw them and welcomed them from a distance. And they admitted that they were aliens and strangers on earth. People who say such things show that they are looking for a country of their own. If they had been thinking of the country they had left, they would have had opportunity to return. Instead, they were longing for a better country—a heavenly one. Therefore God is not ashamed to be called their God, for he has prepared a city for them" (Heb. 11:13-16, NIV).

But what about the recipients of these promises who have died—including people who lived in times of enslavement and captivity, war, poverty, and sickness? For many, life was short, hard, and sometimes cruel. Did these poor people ever live to see peace and prosperity, a reign of righteousness, or the end of wickedness?

No.

As you read Hebrews 11:13-16 in the margin, underline phrases some might consider to be negative circumstances for these saints. Circle phrases that indicate positive outcomes.

The "country of their own" spoken of in Hebrews 11 is a real country, with a real capital city, the New Jerusalem. It is an actual place where these "aliens and strangers on earth" will ultimately live in actual bodies. If the promises God made to them were promises regarding earth (and they were), then the heavenly "country of their own" must ultimately include earth. The fulfillment of these prophecies requires exactly what Scripture elsewhere promises—a resurrection of God's people and God's earth.

What thrilled these expectant believers was not that God would rule in Heaven—He already did. Their hope was that one day He would rule on earth, removing sin, death, suffering, poverty, and heartache. They believed the Messiah would come and bring Heaven to earth. He would make God's will be done on earth as it is in Heaven.

It's commonly taught that the Old Testament concept of Heaven is stunted. However, though it's certainly true that very little is said about the intermediate Heaven, where believers go when they die, the Old Testament actually says a great deal about the eternal Heaven. Unfortunately, we often don't realize it. Why? Because when we read passages about a future earthly kingdom, we assume they don't refer to Heaven. But because God will dwell with His people on the New Earth, these Scripture passages do refer to Heaven.

"But your dead will live; their bodies will rise. You who dwell in the dust, wake up and shout for joy. ... the earth will give birth to her dead" (Isa. 26:19). Just as Adam was made from the dust of the earth, we will be remade from the dust to which we returned at death. God's people are not looking for deliverance from earth, but deliverance on earth. That's exactly what we will find after our bodily resurrection.

DAY TWO

The Question of the Millennium

Many have reduced the coming reign of Christ on earth to a thousand year millennial kingdom on the old earth. Consequently, they have failed to understand the biblical promise of an eternal reign on the New Earth. Because of this, it's necessary for us to take a closer look at the millennium, which has been the subject of considerable debate throughout church history.

Revelation 20 refers six times to the millennium. As you read Revelation 20:1-8 in your Bible, record next to each description below the verse where it is found.

- **The devil is bound for a thousand years. Verse ___**
- **For a thousand years, the nations are no longer deceived. Verse ___**
- **The saints come to life and reign with Christ for a thousand years. Verse ___**
- **The rest of the dead don't come to life until after the thousand years are ended. Verse ___**
- **The saints will be priests and kings for a thousand years. Verse ___**
- **Satan will be loosed at the end of the thousand years, and he will prompt a final human rebellion against God. Verses ___**

Theologians differ over whether the millennium should be understood as a literal thousand-year reign and when it will occur in relation to the second coming of Christ.

From a premillennial viewpoint, the millennium will be a literal thousand-year reign of Christ, which will begin immediately upon His return when He defeats His enemies in the battle of Armageddon. During these thousand years, God's promises of the Messiah's earthly reign will be fulfilled. Redeemed Jews will live in their homeland, and (according to some teachings) the church will govern the world with Christ. The millennium will end with a final rebellion, and the old earth will be replaced by, or transformed into, the New Earth.

From an amillennial viewpoint, the millennium isn't a literal thousand years, nor is it a future state. Rather, the events depicted in Revelation 20:3-7 are happening right now as Christ's church reigns with Him over the earth, in victorious triumph empowered by His death and resurrection. The saints rule over the earth from the present Heaven, where they dwell with Christ.

Theologians who hold to amillennial or premillennial viewpoints differ on specific details even within their own camps. For instance, according to dispensational premillennialism, the rapture will occur prior to the tribulation, and both will occur prior to the final return of Christ to earth. According to historic premillennialism, the rapture is an inseparable part of Christ's single, physical return to earth, which will occur after the tribulation.[1]

Both premillennialism and amillennialism have many biblical points in their favor. I personally believe there will be a literal thousand-year reign of Christ on the present earth (though I'm not dogmatic on this point), but I also understand and respect the strong interpretive arguments that have been made in support of amillennialism.

What's your personal view of the millennium?
___ I hold the premillennial viewpoint.
___ I'm more amillennial.
___ I have no idea what any of this is about.
___ I don't think it really matters in the long run.

Although the millennium is a subject of interest to many, it's not the subject of this study. I mention it only to point out that our beliefs about the millennium need not affect our view of the New Earth. The millennium question relates to whether the old earth will end after the return of Christ or a thousand years later after the end of the millennium. But regardless of when the old earth ends, the central fact is that the New Earth will begin. The Bible is emphatic that God's ultimate kingdom and our final home will not be on the old earth but on the New Earth, where at last

Regardless of when the old earth ends, the central fact is that the New Earth will begin.

God's original design will be fulfilled and enjoyed forever—not just for a thousand years. Hence, no matter how differently we may view the millennium, we can still embrace a common theology of the New Earth.

DAY THREE

The Promised New World

A dominant theme in Old Testament prophecies involves God's plan for an earthly kingdom of righteousness. This pertains to the earth in general and Jerusalem in particular. Isaiah, for example, repeatedly anticipates this coming new world. The Messiah "will reign on David's throne and over his kingdom ... forever" (Isa. 9:7). David's throne was an earthly one, with an earthly past and an earthly future.

In Isaiah 11:1-10, we're told of the Messiah's mission to earth: "He will defend the poor and the exploited. He will rule against the wicked and destroy them" (v. 4). With the lifting of the curse, the Messiah will bring peace to the animal kingdom: "The wolf will live with the lamb, the leopard will lie down with the goat" (v. 6). (This fulfills the deliverance spoken of in Romans 8.) Isaiah says there will be no harm or destruction in Jerusalem (v. 9). The Messiah "will stand as a banner for the peoples," and "the nations will rally to him" (v. 10). His "place of rest will be glorious" (v. 10). (This anticipates Rev. 21–22.)

Where will this happen? Not "up there" in a distant Heaven, but "down here" on earth, in Jerusalem. Isaiah 60 speaks of the city gates always being open because there are no longer any enemies. In words nearly identical to those of John concerning the New Earth (Rev. 21:24-26), it speaks of nations and kings bringing in their wealth. It tells of God's light replacing the sun's and promises that "your days of sorrow will end" (Isa. 60:19-20)—two prophecies clearly fulfilled in Revelation.

Compare Isaiah 60 with Revelation 21:23-26 (in the margin of page 138) by recording the promise that occurs in both passages:

SCRIPTURE

23. "The city does not need the sun or the moon to shine on it, because God's glory illuminates it, and its lamp is the Lamb.
24. The nations will walk in its light, and the kings of the earth will bring their glory into it.
25. Each day its gates will never close because it will never be night there.
26. They will bring the glory and honor of the nations into it"
(Rev. 21:23-26, HCSB).

Isaiah 60:5-7,13 and Revelation 21:26 _____

_____

_____

Isaiah 60:11 and Revelation 21:24 _____

_____

_____

Isaiah 60:11 and Revelation 21:25 _____

_____

_____

Isaiah 60:19 and Revelation 21:23 _____

_____

_____

It is common for prophetic statements to have partial fulfillment in one era and complete fulfillment in another. It may be that these passages will have a partial and initial fulfillment in a literal millennium, explaining why the passages contain a few allusions to death, which is incompatible with the New Earth. But, in context, these prophecies go far beyond a temporary kingdom on an earth that is still infected by sin, curse, and death, and that ends with judgment and destruction. They speak of an eternal kingdom, a messianic reign over a renewed earth that lasts forever, on which sin, curse, and death have no place at all.

What prophecy is repeated in both Isaiah 66:22-23 and Philippians 2:9-11? _____

_____

_____

We should expect Isaiah's prophecies about the Messiah's second coming and the New Earth to be literally fulfilled because his detailed prophecies regarding the Messiah's first coming were literally fulfilled (e.g., Isa. 52:13; 53:4-12). When Jesus spoke to His disciples before ascending to Heaven, He said it was not for them to know when He would restore God's kingdom on earth (Acts 1:6-8), but He did not say they wouldn't know if He would restore God's kingdom. After all, restoring the kingdom of God on earth was His ultimate mission.

God has a future plan for the earth and a future plan for Jerusalem. His plan involves an actual kingdom over which He and His people will reign—not merely for a thousand years but forever (Rev. 22:5). It will be the long-delayed but never-derailed fulfillment of God's command for mankind to exercise righteous dominion over the earth.

The earth's death will be no more final than our own. The destruction of the old earth in God's purifying judgment will immediately be followed by its resurrection to new life. Earth's fiery "end" will open straight into a glorious new beginning.

DAY FOUR

Will the New Earth Be Familiar ... Like Home?

When we open our eyes for the first time on the New Earth, will it be unfamiliar? Or will we recognize it as home?

As human beings, we long for home, even as we step out to explore undiscovered new frontiers. We long for the familiarity of the old, even as we crave the innovation of the new. Think of all the things we love that are new: moving into a new house; the smell of a new car; the feel of a new book; the pleasure of a new friend; the enjoyment of a new pet; new presents on Christmas; welcoming a new child or grandchild. We love newness—yet in each case, what is new is attached to something familiar. We don't really like things that are utterly foreign to us. Instead, we appreciate fresh and innovative variations on things that we already know and love. So when we hear that in Heaven we will have new bodies and live on a New Earth, that's how we should understand the word *new*—a restored and perfected version of our familiar bodies and our familiar earth and our familiar relationships.

When the Bible tells us that Heaven is our home, what meanings should we attach to the word *home*?

SCRIPTURE

"My people will live in peaceful dwelling places, in secure homes, in undisturbed places of rest" (Isa. 32:18, NIV).

Jot down in the margin words that come to mind when you hear the word "home." If you do not have positive emotions toward "home" read Isaiah 32:18 in the margin and describe what God intends "home" to be.

Familiarity is one. I have countless pleasurable memories from childhood. When I gaze at the house I grew up in, every room in that house, every inch of that property, reverberates with memories of my father, mother, brother, friends, dogs, cats, frogs, and lizards. When I go past my childhood home, I step back into a place inseparable from who I was and am, inseparable from my family and friends.

A place with loved ones—that's a central quality of home. The hominess of the house I live in now is inseparable from my wife, Nanci, and my daughters, Angela and Karina, who are married and have their own homes but often come to visit. Everything here speaks of time spent with significant people: playing together, talking together, eating together, reading together, crying together, praying together, charting the course of our lives together. Home is where we're with the ones we love.

Heaven will be just like that. We'll be with people we love, and we'll love no one more than Jesus, who purchased with His own blood the real estate of the New Earth. It won't be long before we settle in there. Because we've already lived on earth, I think it will seem from the first that we're coming home. Because we once lived on earth, the New Earth will strike us as very familiar.

Home is a place where we fit right in. It's the place we were made for. Most houses we live in on earth weren't really made just for us. But the New Earth will be.

SCRIPTURE

"Your heart must not be troubled. Believe in God; believe also in Me. In My Father's house are many dwelling places; if not, I would have told you. I am going away to prepare a place for you" (John 14:1-2, HCSB).

Read John 14:1-2 in the margin. What is Jesus doing right now?

———————————————————————

———————————————————————

———————————————————————

What is your job while Jesus is doing His? (v. 1) ——————————

———————————————————————

———————————————————————

———————————————————————

In Heaven, what kind of a place can we expect our Lord to have prepared for us? Because He isn't limited and He loves us even more than we love our children, I think we can expect to find the best place ever made by anyone, for anyone, in the history of the universe. The God who commends hospitality will not be outdone in His hospitality to us.

> The God who commends hospitality will not be outdone in His hospitality to us.

A good carpenter envisions what he wants to build. He plans and designs. Then he does his work, carefully and skillfully, fashioning it to exact specifications. He takes pride in the work he's done and delights in showing it to others. And when he makes something for his bride or his children, he takes special care and delight.

Jesus is the Carpenter from Nazareth. He knows how to build. He's had experience building entire worlds. He's also an expert at repairing what has been damaged—whether people or worlds. He does not consider His creation disposable. This damaged creation cries out to be repaired, and it is His plan to repair it. He's going to remodel the old earth on a grand scale. How great will be the resurrected planet that He calls the New Earth—the one He says will be our home ... and His.

DAY FIVE

Homesick at Home

Do you recall a time when you were away from your earthly home and desperately missed it? Maybe it was when you were off at college or in the military or traveling extensively overseas or needed to move because of a job. Do you remember how your heart ached for home? That's how we should feel about Heaven. We are a displaced people, longing for our home.

Nothing is more often misdiagnosed than our homesickness for Heaven. We think that what we want is sex, drugs, alcohol, a new job, a raise, a doctorate, a spouse, a large-screen television, a new car, a cabin in the woods, a condo in Hawaii. What we really want is the Person we were made for, Jesus, and the place we were made for, Heaven. Nothing less can satisfy us.

Read Hebrews 11:8-10. What are reasons Abraham might have been homesick for his former earthly home? _____

_____

_____

_____

_____

_____

Yet, where was he looking for ultimate satisfaction? _____

_____

_____

In his discussion of Christian orthodoxy, G. K. Chesterton wrote, "The modern philosopher had told me again and again that I was in the right place, and I had still felt depressed even in acquiescence. ... When I heard that I was in the wrong place ... my soul sang for joy, like a bird in spring. I knew now ... why I could feel homesick at home."[2]

I like Chesterton's picture of feeling homesick at home. We can say, "Heaven will be our eternal home," or "Earth will be our eternal home," but we shouldn't say, "Heaven, not earth, will be our eternal home," because the Heaven in which we'll live will be centered on the New Earth.

We get tired of ourselves, of others, of sin and suffering and crime and death. Yet we love the earth, don't we? I love the spaciousness of the night sky over the desert. I love the coziness of sitting next to Nanci on the couch in front of the fireplace, blanket over us and dog snuggled next to us. These experiences are not Heaven—but they are foretastes of Heaven. What we love about this life are the things that resonate with the life we were made for. The things we love are not merely the best this life has to offer—they are previews of the greater life to come.

Find Zephaniah in your Bible and slowly read 3:14-20. Spend time talking with God, telling Him how much you love Him, how homesick you are for Him, and how thankful you are for home.

1. Wayne Grudem, *Systematic Theology: An Introduction to Biblical Doctrine* (Grand Rapids: Zondervan, 1994), 1111-14.
2. G. K. Chesterton, *Orthodoxy* (Chicago: Thomas More Association, 1985), 99-100.

LEADER GUIDE

To the Leader
Although you don't
want to spend your
entire time discussing
the millennium, you do
want to be prepared to
explain it adequately. For
more explanation of the
millennial views, read the
HCSB Study Bible Notes
for Revelation 20:1-8 on
mystudybible.com and/
or the *Holman Illustrated
Bible Dictionary* article
on "Millennium" (which
can also be found on
mystudybible.com).
As the class briefly
discusses this topic,
make certain every par-
ticipant feels his or her
view of the millennium
is respected.

During the Session

1. Ask participants to identify topics sure to raise blood pressure because people have differing opinions about them or they are confusing. Then ask that they identify topics that make people feel happy and peaceful. State that the class is going to examine end times, a subject matter that often causes disagreement or confusion. But you'll also address the joyful and peaceful topic of "home."

2. Assert that God has promised His people a home. Read Isaiah 32:18 (printed in the margin of Day Four, p. 140). To examine some of those promises, complete the first activity of Day One (p. 133). (You may want to do this in teams.) Point out the partial and complete fulfillment of Old Testament prophecies (see Day Three) to explain why death is mentioned in Isaiah 65. Read the first paragraph on page 134. Remark that these saints surely questioned where and when their deliverance was coming. Evaluate how Hebrews 11:13-16 answers that question. Ask: *Would God promise something and not deliver it fully? Would He promise a city and country and instead deliver some nebulous spirit realm where His people float around with nothing to do?* (These questions may be rhetoric or participants may want to discuss them.) Read Alcorn's statement: "The fulfillment of these prophecies requires exactly what Scripture … promises—a resurrection of God's people and God's earth" (p. 134). ☊

3. State that our understanding of when that final resurrection will occur is complicated by the biblical teaching of the millennium. Complete the first activity of Day Two (p. 135). Organize two teams to explore the information in Day Two and be prepared to briefly explain premillennialism or amillennialism. Allow teams to report. Invite responses to the second activity of Day Two (p. 136). Ask: *Why shouldn't our view of the millennium affect our view of Heaven?* Declare: *We can have differing views and still end up at the same place—home.* ☊

4. State that the Old Testament prophesies a home in an earthly kingdom over which Christ will reign forever. Use the remarks and activities of

Day Three to examine the parallels between Isaiah's prophecies and the details of the New Earth in Revelation. Alcorn declares this won't happen "up there" but "down here" on the New Earth. (Draw attention to the posters you created in the week of October 23 distinguishing between the present and eternal Heavens.) Consider why believers should expect Old Testament prophecies of the New Earth to be literally fulfilled.

5. Alcorn speaks in the last paragraph of Day Three of earth's death, destruction, and fiery end (p. 139). Peter spoke of what will happen to this present earth in 2 Peter 3:3-10. Invite someone to read that passage. Point out that this is the same Peter who declared in Acts 3:21 that God will restore everything. The flood was cataclysmic, but it did not destroy the earth; it just pushed the reset button. This next time God will push the restore, redeem, and renew button. God's fiery judgment will consume the bad, refine the good, and transform this present earth into His original intention of a wonderful home for His people.

6. Invite responses to the questions in the first paragraph of Day Four (p. 139). Ask: *What do you love about new things? Would you enjoy the new if there was never anything familiar? Explain.* How should we understand the word "new" as it relates to our new bodies on a New Earth? (See end of second paragraph of Day Four, p. 139.) When the Bible tells us Heaven is our home, what meanings should we attach to "home?" Discuss the second activity of Day Four (p. 140). Request learners consider a time they prepared their home for someone special and state what they would have done if they had had no limitations. Consider what kind of home an unlimited Christ must be preparing. Ask what believers are to be doing while Jesus is preparing. Refer back to Hebrews 11 where the saints were commended for trusting that God would deliver them safely to a wonderful home.

7. Inquire: *What do you love most about your home on this earth? How is it possible to be "homesick at home?" When do you get the most homesick for home on the New Earth?* Read Zephaniah 3:20. State: *We don't know what "that time" is, but we can know without a doubt if we have placed our faith in Christ that He will bring us home. What do you most look forward to when you think about going home?* Close in prayer. ♥

Celebrating Our Relationship with God

DAY ONE

What Will It Mean to See God?

If I were dealing with aspects of Heaven in their order of importance, I would have begun with a chapter about God and our eternal relationship with Him. However, I thought it was first necessary to establish a clear picture of our physical, resurrected life on the New Earth. If we don't base our perspective of Heaven on a clear understanding of our coming bodily resurrection and the truth about the physical nature of the New Earth, our concept of being with God will be more like that of Eastern mysticism than of biblical Christianity.

Read Psalm 27:8 and Revelation 22:4 in the margin. What did the psalmist seek? _____

What will God's servants on the New Earth see?_____

_____

_____

SCRIPTURE

"My heart says this about You, 'You are to seek My face.' LORD, I will seek Your face" (Ps. 27:8, HCSB).

"They will see His face" (Rev. 22:4, HCSB).

To see God's face is the loftiest of all aspirations—though sadly, for most of us, it's not at the top of our wish list. (If we understand what it means, it will be.)

To be told we'll see God's face is shocking to anyone who understands God's transcendence and inapproachability. In ancient Israel, only the high priest could go into the holy of holies, and he but once a year. Even then, according to tradition, a rope was tied around the priest's ankle in case he died while inside the holy of holies. Why? Well, God struck down Uzzah for touching the ark of the covenant (2 Sam. 6:7). Who would volunteer to go into the holy of holies to pull out the high priest if God slew him?

When Moses said to God, "Show me your glory," God responded, "'I will cause all my goodness to pass in front of you. ... But,' he said, 'you cannot see my face...'" (Ex. 33:18-23).

Read Exodus 33:18-23 in your Bible. What did God allow Moses to see? Why? _____

_____

_____

_____

Moses saw God but not God's face. The New Testament says that God "lives in unapproachable light, whom no one has seen or can see" (1 Tim. 6:16). To see God's face was utterly unthinkable.

That's why, when we're told in Revelation 22:4 that we'll see God's face, it should astound us. For this to happen, it would require that we undergo something radical between now and then. The obstacles to seeing God are daunting: "without holiness no one will see the Lord" (Heb. 12:14). It's only because we'll be fully righteous in Christ, completely sinless, that we'll be able to see God and live.

Not only will we see His face and live, but we will likely wonder if we ever lived before we saw His face!

Not only will we see His face and live, but we will likely wonder if we ever lived before we saw His face! To see God will be our greatest joy, the joy by which all others will be measured.

In Heaven, the barriers between redeemed human beings and God will forever be gone. To look into God's eyes will be to see what we've always longed to see: the Person who made us for His own good pleasure. Seeing God will be like seeing everything else for the first time. Why? Because not only will we see God, He will be the lens through which we see everything else—people, ourselves, and the events of this life.

What is the essence of eternal life? "That they may know you, the only true God, and Jesus Christ, whom you have sent" (John 17:3). Our primary joy in Heaven will be knowing and seeing God. Every other joy will be derivative, flowing from the fountain of our relationship with God.

What do you think you'll see in God's eyes when you see Him face-to-face?_____

_____

_____

_____

DAY TWO

What Will It Mean for God to Dwell Among Us?

Consider this statement: "God Himself will be with them" (Rev. 21:3, hcsb). Why does it emphatically say "God Himself"? Because God won't merely send us a delegate. He will actually come to live among us on the New Earth.

God's glory will be the air we breathe, and we'll always breathe deeper to gain more of it. In the new universe, we'll never be able to travel far enough to leave God's presence. If we could, we'd never want to. However great the wonders of Heaven, God Himself is Heaven's greatest prize.

In Heaven we'll at last be freed of self-righteousness and self-deceit. We'll no longer question God's goodness; we'll see it, savor it, enjoy it, and declare it to our companions. Surely we will wonder how we ever could have doubted His goodness. For then our faith will be sight—we shall see God.

Not only will God come to dwell with us on earth, He will also bring with Him the New Jerusalem, an entire city of people, structures, streets, walls, rivers, and trees, that is now in the present, intermediate Heaven.

Read in your Bible Revelation 21:10-14 and 22:1-5. Write the verse where you find reference to the following entities that will be in Heaven:

city _____

people _____

walls _____

streets _____

rivers _____

trees _____

If you've ever seen a house being relocated, you appreciate what a massive undertaking it is. God will relocate an entire city—Heaven's capital city, the New Jerusalem—from Heaven to earth. It's a vast complex containing, perhaps, hundreds of millions of residences. He will bring with it Heaven's human inhabitants and angels as well.

It appears that God has already fashioned the New Jerusalem: "He has prepared a city for them" (Heb. 11:16). It doesn't say that God will prepare a city or even that He is preparing it, but that He has prepared it. This suggests that the New Jerusalem, complete or nearly complete, is already there in the present Heaven. When God fashions the New Earth, He will relocate the city from Heaven to the New Earth. It's possible that those in the present Heaven are already living in it. Or it may be set aside, awaiting simultaneous habitation by all its occupants when transferred to the New Earth. Imagine the thrill of beholding and exploring God's city together!

The presence of God is the essence of Heaven (just as the absence of God is the essence of Hell). Because God is beautiful beyond measure, if we knew nothing more than that Heaven was God's dwelling place, it would be more than enough. The best part of life on the New Earth will be enjoying God's presence, having Him actually dwell among us (Rev. 21:3-4). Just as the holy of holies contained the dazzling presence of God in ancient Israel, so will the New Jerusalem contain His presence—but on a much larger scale—on the New Earth. The holy of holies in the temple at Jerusalem was a perfect thirty-foot cube. The New Jerusalem itself will be a perfect cube, one that stretches 1,400 miles in each direction (Rev. 21:16).

In the New Jerusalem, there will be no temple (Rev. 21:22). Everyone will be allowed unimpeded access into God's presence. "Blessed are those who … may go through the gates into the city" (Rev. 22:14).

Heaven's greatest miracle will be our access to God. In the New Jerusalem, we will be able to come physically, through wide open gates, to God's throne.

> The presence of God is the essence of Heaven.

Read the passages from Hebrews in the margin. What can you do even now? _____

_____

_____

DAY THREE

How Can Millions of People All Be with Jesus and Receive Personal Attention?

SCRIPTURE

"Let us then approach the throne of grace with confidence, so that we may receive mercy and find grace to help us in our time of need" (Heb. 4:16, NIV).

"Therefore, brothers, since we have confidence to enter the Most Holy Place by the blood of Jesus ... let us draw near to God with a sincere heart in full assurance of faith, having our hearts sprinkled to cleanse us from a guilty conscience and having our bodies washed with pure water" (Heb. 10:19,22, NIV).

After the first edition of this book, this question was one of the most frequently asked. It's worth considering.

Though it's possible we may cover vast distances at immense speeds in God's new universe, I don't believe we'll be capable of being two places at once. Why? Because we'll still be finite. Only God is infinite.

Because the resurrected Christ is both man and God, the issue of whether He can be in more than one place at the same time involves a paradox not only in the future, but also in the present.

On the one hand, Jesus is a man, and man is finite and limited to one location. On the other hand, Jesus is God, and God is infinite and omnipresent. In a sense, then, one of these truths has to yield somewhat to the other. I suggest that perhaps Christ's humanity defined the extent of His presence in His first coming and life on earth (humanity thereby trumping deity by limiting omnipresence). But Christ's deity may well define the extent of His presence in His second coming and life on the New Earth (deity thereby trumping the normal human inability to be in two places at once). Jesus has and always will have a single resurrected body, in keeping with His humanity. Yet that body glorified may allow Him a far greater expression of His divine attributes than during His life and ministry here on earth.

SCRIPTURE

"Let us fix our eyes on Jesus, the author and perfecter of our faith, who for the joy set before him endured the cross, scorning its shame, and sat down at the right hand of the throne of God" (Heb. 12:2, NIV).

"I pray that out of his glorious riches he may strengthen you with power through his Spirit in your inner being, so that Christ may dwell in your hearts through faith" (Eph. 3:16-17, NIV).

"I have been crucified with Christ and I no longer live, but Christ lives in me" (Gal. 2:20, NIV).

Since we can accurately say that Jesus' functioning as a man does not prohibit Him from being God, we must also say that Jesus' functioning as God does not prohibit Him from being a man. So, although we cannot conceive exactly how it could happen, I believe it's entirely possible that Jesus could in the future remain a man while fully exercising the attributes of God, including, at least in some sense, omnipresence.

Don't we already see that now?

Where is Christ according to Hebrews 12:2? _____

_____

And yet where else is Christ according to Ephesians 3:16-17 and Galatians 2:20? _____

_____

_____

Just before dying, Stephen saw Him in Heaven (Acts 7:55). Jesus will remain there until He returns to the earth. In terms of His human body, Christ is in one location, and only one.

But despite His fixed location at God's right hand, Jesus is here now, with each of us, just as He promised to be (Matt. 28:20). He dwells in our hearts, living within us (Eph. 3:17; Gal. 2:20). If even now, in this sin-stained world, He indwells those who are saints and yet sinners, how much more will He be able to indwell us in the world to come when no sin shall separate us from Him? That indwelling will in no way be obscured by sin.

On the New Earth, isn't it likely we might regularly hear Him speak to us directly as He dwells in and with us, wherever we are? Prayer might be an unhindered two-way conversation, whether we are hundreds of miles away in another part of the New Jerusalem, thousands of miles away on another part of the New Earth, or thousands of light years away in the new universe.

Consider the promise that when Christ returns "every eye will see him" (Rev. 1:7). How is that physically possible? By the projection of His image? But every eye will see Him, not merely His image. Will He be in more than one place at one time?

If God took on human form any number of times, as recorded in Scripture, couldn't Christ choose to take on a form to manifest Himself to us at a distant place? If He did that, might He not take on a temporary form very similar in appearance to His actual physical form, which may at that moment be sitting on the throne in the New Jerusalem? Might Jesus appear to us and walk with us in a temporary but tangible form that is an expression of His real body? Or might the one body of Jesus be simultaneously present with His people in a million places?

Might we walk with Jesus (not just spiritually, but also physically) while millions of others are also walking with him? Might we not be able to touch His hand or embrace Him or spend a long afternoon privately conversing with Him—not just with His spirit, but His whole person?

It may defy our logic, but God is capable of doing far more than we imagine. Being with Christ is the very heart of Heaven, so we should be confident that we will have unhindered access to Him.

To what do you think the benediction in Ephesians 3:20-21 (in the margin) refers?
___ **what God can do now on earth**
___ **what God will do in Heaven**
___ **both of the above**

DAY FOUR

Will God Serve Us?

SCRIPTURE

"Now to Him who is able to do above and beyond all that we ask or think according to the power that works in us—to Him be glory in the church and in Christ Jesus to all generations, forever and ever. Amen" (Eph. 3:20-21, HCSB).

Jesus said, "It will be good for those servants whose master finds them watching when he comes. I tell you the truth, he will dress himself to serve, will have them recline at the table and will come and wait on them" (Luke 12:37).

This is an amazing passage. Jesus says that the Master will do something culturally unthinkable—become a servant to His servants. Why? Because He loves them, and also out of appreciation for their loyalty and service to Him. The King becomes a servant, making His servants kings! Notice that He won't merely command His other servants to serve them. He will do it Himself.

We will be in Heaven only because "the Son of Man did not come to be served, but to serve, and to give his life as a ransom for many" (Matt. 20:28). We must assent to Christ's service for us (John 13:8). But even in Heaven, it appears, Jesus will sometimes serve us. What greater and more amazing reward could be ours in the new universe than to have Jesus choose to serve us?

How do you feel about the idea of Jesus serving you in Heaven?
____ **No way!**
____ **I'm struggling with it.**
____ **I'm overwhelmed at the thought.**
____ **Your own thought:** _____
_____
_____

SCRIPTURE

"The LORD of Hosts will prepare a feast for all the peoples on this mountain—a feast of aged wine, choice meat, finely aged wine. On this mountain He will destroy the burial shroud, the shroud over all the peoples, the sheet covering all the nations; He will destroy death forever. The Lord GOD will wipe away the tears from every face and remove His people's disgrace from the whole earth, for the LORD has spoken. On that day it will be said, "Look, this is our God; we have waited for Him, and He has saved us. This is the LORD; we have waited for Him. Let us rejoice and be glad in His salvation" (Isa. 25:6-9, HCSB).

If it was our idea that God would serve us, it would be blasphemy. But it's His idea. As husbands serve their wives and parents serve their children, God desires to serve us.

As you read Isaiah 25:6-9 in the margin, underline all the ways God will serve His people.

What is to be our response to such a powerful, yet serving, God?
_____
_____
_____
_____

God will be the chef—He'll prepare us a meal. In Heaven, God will overwhelm us with His humility and His grace.

Both God the Father and God the Son are portrayed as reigning on thrones in Heaven. But what will be the Holy Spirit's role? The answer isn't spelled out in detail, but we can surmise that He'll be involved in creating the new Heavens and New Earth (Gen. 1:2; Isa. 32:15). He may continue to indwell believers (John 16:7). He'll empower us to rule wisely with Christ (Deut. 34:9). He may still move our hearts to glorify and worship the Father and the Son (John 16:14; Rev. 19:1-10). He'll continue forever as their companion in the triune Godhead (Gen. 1:26; Heb. 9:14).

DAY FIVE

How Will We Worship God?

Have you ever—in prayer or corporate worship or during a walk on the beach—for a few moments experienced the very presence of God? It's a tantalizing encounter, yet for most of us it tends to disappear quickly in the distractions of life. What will it be like to behold God's face and never be distracted by lesser things?

Most people know that we'll worship God in Heaven. But they don't grasp how thrilling that will be. Multitudes of God's people—of every nation, tribe, people, and language—will gather to sing praise to God for his greatness, wisdom, power, grace, and mighty work of redemption (Rev. 5:13-14). Overwhelmed by His magnificence, we will fall on our faces in unrestrained happiness and say, "Praise and glory and wisdom and thanks and honor and power and strength be to our God for ever and ever. Amen!" (Rev. 7:9-12).

People of the world are always striving to celebrate—they just lack ultimate reasons to celebrate (and therefore find lesser reasons). As Christians, we have those reasons—our relationship with Jesus and the promise of Heaven. "Now the dwelling of God is with men, and he will live with them. They will be his people, and God himself will be with them and be their God" (Rev. 21:3). Does this excite you? If it doesn't, you're not thinking correctly.

Will we always be engaged in worship? Yes and no. If we have a narrow view of worship, the answer is no. But if we have a broad view of worship, the answer is yes.

Will Heaven be one unending church service? Read Revelation 21:22 in the margin. Check your answer and explain:

SCRIPTURE

"I did not see a temple in the city, because the Lord God Almighty and the Lamb are its temple" Rev. 21:22, NIV).

____ **Yes, because** _____

_____

_____

_____

____ **No, because** _____

_____

_____

_____

Will we always be on our faces at Christ's feet, worshiping Him? No, because Scripture says we'll be doing many other things—living in dwelling places, eating and drinking, reigning with Christ, and working for Him. Scripture depicts people standing, walking, traveling in and out of the city, and gathering at feasts. When doing these things, we won't be on our faces before Christ. Nevertheless, all that we do will be an act of worship. We'll enjoy full and unbroken fellowship with Christ. At times this will crescendo into greater heights of praise as we assemble with the multitudes who are also worshiping Him.

In Heaven, worshiping God won't be restricted to a time posted on a sign, telling us when to start and stop. It will permeate our lives, energize our bodies, and fuel our imaginations.

> **"Rejoice always! Pray constantly, give thanks in everything; for this is God's will for you in Christ Jesus" (1 Thess. 5:16-18, HCSB). How can you do the following, even now?**
> **rejoice always**_____
>
> _____
>
> _____
>
> _____
>
> **pray continually**_____
>
> _____
>
> _____
>
> _____
>
> **give thanks in all things** _____
>
> _____
>
> _____
>
> _____

LEADER GUIDE

The best way for learners to catch a glimpse of what it will be like to be with God and worship God forever is to be with and worship with God's people now. Enlist a class member to plan a class fellowship.

Pray about which learners particularly need "God with skin on" and meet that need through meeting them for coffee, giving them a call, sending a card, etc.

Before the Session

Enlist four volunteers to be prepared to read Leviticus 26:11-12, Ezekiel 37:27, 2 Corinthians 6:16, and Revelation 21:3.

During the Session

1. Ask: *How do you stay in contact with loved ones who live far away? Is phoning, e-mailing, and Skyping enough? Why do we sometimes need to physically be with people we love and see their faces?* Remind participants that last week you explored the concept of being homesick for home. Ask if they would agree that a longing for Heaven is really a longing for God and why. Today's study explores five questions (the headings for each day). The first two questions explore the realities of physically being with God and seeing His face.

2. Discuss the first activity of Day One (p. 145). Consider why the statements in both Psalm 27 and Revelation 22 are shocking statements. State that Moses was one of the godliest men who ever lived, yet even he was not allowed to see God's face. Invite someone to read Exodus 33:12-23. Discuss: *What did Moses actually ask to see? How is seeing God's face the same as seeing His glory? Why do you think Moses wanted to see God's glory? Why can no one see God and live? Then why would we even think about wanting to see God's face?* State that David also desired to see God's face. Ask a volunteer to read Psalm 27:4-8. Explore what David was seeking when he sought God's face. Request participants state from Hebrews 12:14 what prevents anyone from seeing God. Ask: *How is perfect holiness possible?* Respond to the margin quote on page 146. Ask: *Why will seeing God be like seeing everything for the first time?* Invite responses to the final activity of Day One (p. 147).

3. Ask what is required for learners to be able to physically be with loved ones who live far away. Declare: *We won't have to leave home to see God; He will be with us.* Request the pre-enlisted volunteers read their verses. Ask what God will bring with Him when He comes to dwell with us. Use the first activity of Day Two (p. 147) to explore the New Jerusalem.

Ask: If we knew nothing else about this eternal Heaven, why would it be enough to know God will live there with us? Evaluate how believers can be with God now.

4. Remark that Days Three through Five explore three questions that arise out of the two realities of seeing God's face and God's dwelling among us. Invite a volunteer to read the title for Day Three. Ask if participants have ever wondered about that. Encourage learners to recall (or look up in their Bibles) what Jesus promised His followers in Matthew 28:20 and John 14:3. Invite them to imagine what it will be like to physically be with Jesus. State: *We can enjoy being with Jesus while millions of others are as well!* Evaluate why it requires faith in Jesus' deity and glorified resurrected body to accept that truth. Discuss the last activity of Day Three (p. 151).

5. Request someone read Day Four's title. Identify from Matthew 20:28 Jesus' purpose for coming to earth. Explain how He gave a powerful demonstration of that purpose when He washed the disciples' feet (John 13). Point out Peter's reaction (v. 8). According to Luke 12:37, Jesus will serve His followers in Heaven. Invite responses to the first activity of Day Four (p. 152). Ask participants if they enjoy serving their loved ones and why. Determine how that helps them understand why God will serve believers in Heaven. Discuss the second activity of Day Four (p. 152). Point out that our appropriate response is worship. Day Five explores how we will worship God in Heaven.

6. Ask: *Why might some think that Heaven will be boring?* Discuss the first activity of Day Five (p. 153). Analyze how learners worship God now at times other than in prayer and worship services. Ask how worship services take them to a deeper level of worship.☻ Explain that even if we won't always be formally worshiping God (as we define it) there will be times of glorious worship. Invite volunteers to read Revelation 5:11-14 and 7:9-12. Ask: *What will be most thrilling about those times of worship to you? Why will spending an eternity with God be anything but boring?* Close in prayer.

Ruling on the New Earth

DAY ONE

What Does God's Eternal Kingdom Involve?

If you were to describe a kingdom, what elements would you include? A king, certainly, and subjects to be ruled, but what else? In order to be rightly described as a kingdom, wouldn't it also have to include territory, a government, and a culture? Why is it, then, that when we think of God's kingdom, we often think only of the King and His subjects, but we leave out the territory and the culture? We spiritualize God's kingdom, perceiving it as otherworldly and intangible. But Scripture tells us otherwise.

When Jesus was on trial, He said to Pilate, "My kingdom is not of this world" (John 18:36). He did not mean that His kingdom wouldn't be on this earth after it is transformed. He meant that His kingdom isn't of this earth as it is now, under the curse. Although Christ's kingdom isn't from the earth, it extends to the earth, and one day it will fully include the earth and be centered on it.

Revelation 5:1-10 depicts a powerful scene in the present Heaven. God the Father, the Ruler of Heaven, sits on the throne with a sealed scroll in His right hand. What's sealed—with seven seals, to avoid any possibility that the document has been tampered with—is the Father's will, His plan for the distribution and management of His estate. In this case, the entitlement of the estate is the earth, which includes its people. God had intended for the world to be ruled by humans. But who will come forward to open the document and receive the inheritance?

Read Revelation 5:1-4 in your Bible. What did John do when God revealed this scene to him and why? _____

_____

_____

Because of human sin, mankind and the earth have been corrupted. No man is worthy to take the role God intended for Adam and his descendants. Adam proved unworthy, as did Abraham, David, and every other person in history. But right when it appears that God's design for mankind and the earth will forever be thwarted, the text continues in high drama: "Then one of the elders said to me, 'Do not weep! See, the Lion of the tribe of Judah, the Root of David, has triumphed. He is able to open the scroll and its seven seals.' Then I saw a Lamb, looking as if it had been slain, standing in the center of the throne, encircled by the four living creatures and the elders. … He came and took the scroll from the right hand of him who sat on the throne. And when he had taken it, the four living creatures and the twenty-four elders fell down before the Lamb. … And they sang a new song: 'You are worthy to take the scroll and to open its seals, because you were slain, and with your blood you purchased men for God from every tribe and language and people and nation'" (Rev. 5:5-9).

SCRIPTURE

"You made them a kingdom and priests to our God, and they will reign on the earth" (Rev. 5:10, HCSB).

Read Revelation 5:10 in the margin. In their song, what did the living creatures declare about Christ's followers? _____

_____

_____

Psalm 2 speaks of Christ ruling "with an iron scepter" and dashing the nations to pieces "like pottery" (v. 9), a reference to the Messiah's return, judgment, and perhaps His millennial reign. But once we enter the new Heavens and New Earth, there's no iron rule or dashing to pieces, for there's no more rebellion, sin, or death. The vanquishing of sin doesn't mean the end of Christ's rule. It means the end of His contested rule and the beginning of His eternally uncontested rule, when He will delegate earthly rule to His co-heirs.

If we understood God's unaltered plan for His people to exercise dominion over the earth, it wouldn't surprise us to find on the New Earth that nations still exist and kings come into the New Jerusalem bringing tribute to the King of kings (Rev. 21:24,26).

DAY TWO

Will We Actually Rule With Christ?

Read the passages in the margin. How is the decree in Revelation 22:5 a direct fulfillment of God's charge to Adam and Eve in Genesis 1:28? _____

_____

_____

_____

_____

SCRIPTURE

"And they [His servants] will reign for ever and ever" (Rev. 22:5, NIV).

"God blessed them and said to them, 'Be fruitful and increase in number; fill the earth and subdue it. Rule over the fish of the sea and the birds of the air and over every living creature that moves on the ground'" (Gen. 1:28, NIV).

God created Adam and Eve to be king and queen over the earth. Their job was to rule the earth, to the glory of God.

They failed.

Jesus Christ is the second Adam, and the church is His bride, the second Eve. Christ is King, the church is His queen. Christ will exercise dominion over all nations of the earth: "He will rule from sea to sea and from the River to the ends of the earth. ... All kings will bow down to him and all nations will serve him" (Ps. 72:8,11). As the new head of the human race, Christ—with His beloved people as His bride and co-rulers—will at last accomplish what was entrusted to Adam and Eve. God's saints will fulfill on the New Earth the role God first assigned to Adam and Eve on the old earth. "They will reign for ever and ever" (Rev. 22:5).

Because I teach on the subject of redeemed humanity ruling the earth, I've had many opportunities to observe people's responses. Often they're surprised to learn that we will reign in eternity over lands, cities, and nations. Many are skeptical—it's a foreign concept that seems fanciful. Nothing demonstrates how far we've distanced ourselves from our biblical calling like our lack of knowledge about our destiny to rule the earth. Why are we so surprised, when it is spoken of throughout the Old Testament and repeatedly reaffirmed in the New Testament?

Because crowns are the primary symbol of ruling, every mention of crowns as rewards is a reference to our ruling with Christ. In His parables, Jesus speaks of our ruling over cities (Luke 19:17). Paul addresses the subject of Christians ruling as if it were Theology 101.

Read 1 Corinthians 6:2-3 in the margin. Paul felt every believer should be well aware that _____

_____

_____ .

When we consider that mankind's reign on the earth is introduced in the first chapters of the Bible, mentioned throughout the Old Testament, discussed by Jesus in the Gospels, by Paul in the Epistles, and repeated by John in the Bible's final chapters, it is remarkable that we would fail to see it. Remembering again that a "crown" speaks of ruling authority, consider the following examples from one small portion of Scripture, Revelation 2–5:

"Be faithful, even to the point of death, and I will give you the crown of life" (2:10).

"To him who overcomes and does my will to the end, I will give authority over the nations" (2:26).

"I am coming soon. Hold on to what you have, so that no one will take your crown" (3:11).

"To him who overcomes, I will give the right to sit with me on my throne, just as I overcame and sat down with my Father on his throne" (3:21).

"The twenty-four elders fall down before him who sits on the throne … They lay their crowns before the throne" (4:10).

"[You] have redeemed us to God by Your blood out of every tribe and tongue and people and nation, and have made us kings and priests to our God; and we shall reign on the earth" (5:9-10, nkjv).

In these verses, who does God say will reign? _____

_____

Where will they reign? _____

_____

People of every tribe and language and people and nation will reign on earth, not in some intangible heavenly realm. Where on earth? Likely with people of their own tribe, language, and nation—cultural distinctives that we're told still exist on the New Earth (Rev. 21:24,26; 22:2).

Wayne Grudem states that "when the author of Hebrews says that we do 'not yet' see everything in subjection to man (Heb. 2:8), he implies that all things will eventually be subject to us, under the kingship of the man Christ Jesus. … This will fulfill God's original plan to have everything in the world subject to the human beings that he had made. In this sense, then, we will 'inherit the earth' (Matt. 5:5) and reign over it as God originally intended."[1]

DAY THREE

Should We Want to Rule?

The government of the New Earth won't be a democracy. It won't be majority rule, and it won't be driven by opinion polls. Instead, every citizen of Heaven will have an appointed role, one that fulfills him or her and contributes to the whole. No one will "fall through the cracks" in God's kingdom. No one will feel worthless or insignificant.

When I write and speak on this subject, people often respond, "But I don't want to rule. That's not my idea of Heaven."

Can you relate with that sentiment? Why? _____

_____

_____

_____

Well, it's *God's* idea of Heaven.

We are part of God's family. Ruling the universe is the family business. To want no part of it is to want no part of our Father. It may sound spiritual to say we don't care to rule, but because God's the One who wants us to rule, the spiritual response is to be interested in His plans and purposes.

Whom will we rule? Other people. Angels. If God wishes, He may create new beings for us to rule. Who will rule over us? Other people.

There will be a social hierarchy of government, but there's no indication of a relational hierarchy. There will be no pride, envy, boasting, or anything sin-related. Our differences will be a manifestation of God's creativity. As we're different in race, nationality, gender, personality, gifting, and passions, so we'll be different in positions of service.

All of us will have some responsibility in which we serve God. Scripture teaches that our service for Him now on earth will be evaluated to help determine how we'll serve Him on the New Earth. The humble servant will be put in charge of much, whereas the one who lords it over others in the present world will have power taken away: "For everyone who exalts himself will be humbled, and he who humbles himself will be exalted" (Luke 14:11). If we serve faithfully on the present earth, God will give us permanent management positions on the New Earth. "Whoever can be trusted with very little can also be trusted with much" (Luke 16:10). The Owner has His eye on us—if we prove faithful, He'll be pleased to entrust more to us.

We've been conditioned to associate governing with self-promoting arrogance, corruption, inequality, and inefficiency. But these are perversions, not inherent properties of leadership. Ruling involves responsibility—perhaps that's why some people don't look forward to it. Some people live in anticipation of retirement, when responsibilities will be removed. Why would they want to take on an eternal task of governing? But what they think they want now and what they'll really want as resurrected beings—with strong bodies and minds in a society untouched by sin—may be quite different.

Imagine responsibility, service, and leadership that's pure joy. The responsibility that God will entrust to us as a reward can only be good for us, and we'll find delight in it.

Of course, not all positions of responsibility over others involve people. Adam and Eve governed animals before there were any other people. Some of us may be granted the privilege of caring for animals. Perhaps some will care for forests. Ruling will likely involve the management of all of God's creation, not just people.

Perhaps God will offer us choices of where we might want to serve Him. On the New Earth, we'll do what we want, but we'll want what God wants, and that will bring us our greatest joy.

Some of the most qualified people to lead in Heaven will be those who don't want to lead now. Some who are natural leaders here but have not been faithful will not be leaders in Heaven.

Read Matthew 5:5 in the margin. Check who will inherit the earth.
___ the proud and confident
___ the meek and gentle

SCRIPTURE

"Blessed are the meek, for they will inherit the earth" (Matt. 5:5, NIV).

And even the meek will be stripped of their wrong motives and the temptation to exploit others. We'll have no more skepticism and disillusionment about government. Why? Because we'll be governed by Christlike rulers, and all of us will be under the grand and gracious government of Christ Himself.

DAY FOUR

Looking Forward to What God Has for Us

Read Matthew 25:23 in the margin. How did the master reward the faithful servant?
___ Sent him on a 3-week cruise
___ Gave him 500 shares of stock
___ Gave him a corner office
___ Gave him more responsibility

SCRIPTURE

"His master said to him, 'Well done, good and faithful servant. You have been faithful over a little; I will set you over much. Enter into the joy of your master'" (Matt. 25:23, ESV).

The idea of entering into the Master's joy is a telling picture of Heaven. It's not simply that being with the Master produces joy in us, though certainly it will. Rather, it's that our Master Himself is joyful. He takes joy in Himself, in His children, and in His creation. His joy is contagious. Once we're liberated from the sin that blocks us from God's joy and our own, we'll enter into His joy. Joy will be the very air we breathe. The Lord is inexhaustible—therefore His joy is inexhaustible.

God is grooming us for leadership. He's watching to see how we demonstrate our faithfulness. He does that through His apprenticeship program, one that prepares us for Heaven. Christ is not simply preparing a place for us; He is preparing us for that place.

We all have dreams but often don't see them realized. We become discouraged and lose hope. But as Christ's apprentices, we must learn certain disciplines. Apprentices in training must work hard and study hard to prepare for the next test or challenge. Apprentices may wish for three weeks of vacation or more pay to pursue outside interests. But the Master may see that these would not lead to success. He may override His apprentices' desires in order that they might learn perspective and patience, which will serve them well in the future. While the young apprentices experience the death of their dreams, the Master is shaping them to dream greater dreams that they will one day live out on the New Earth with enhanced wisdom, skill, appreciation, and joy.

Through the challenges you now face, what dreams might God be preparing you to live out on the New Earth?

Think about the question above, then record the dreams that God might be preparing you to live out on the New Earth. _____

_____

_____

_____

_____

_____

_____

_____

_____

DAY FIVE

Service as a Reward

Read Revelation 7:14-15. How will those coming out of the tribulation be rewarded? _____

_____

_____

_____

SCRIPTURE

"These are the ones coming out of the great tribulation. They washed their robes and made them white in the blood of the Lamb. For this reason they are before the throne of God, and they serve Him day and night in His sanctuary. The One seated on the throne will shelter them" (Rev. 7:14-15, HCSB).

Those coming out of the great tribulation will be specially rewarded by being given a place "before the throne of God," where they will "serve him day and night" (Rev. 7:14-15). The Master rewards His faithful servants not by taking away responsibilities but by giving them greater ones.

Service is a reward, not a punishment. This idea is foreign to people who dislike their work and only put up with it until retirement. We think that faithful work should be rewarded by a vacation for the rest of our lives. But God offers us something very different: more work, more responsibilities, and increased opportunities, along with greater abilities, resources, wisdom, and empowerment. We will have sharp minds, strong bodies, clear purpose, and unabated joy. The more we serve Christ now, the greater our capacity will be to serve Him in Heaven.

Reigning over cities will certainly not be "having nothing to do." I believe that those who rule cities on the New Earth will have leisure (rest) and will fully enjoy it, but they will have plenty to do.

Will everyone be given the opportunity to rule in the new universe? The apostle Paul said that eternal rewards are available "not only to me, but also to all who have longed for his appearing" (2 Tim. 4:8). "The Lord will reward everyone for whatever good he does, whether he is slave or free" (Eph. 6:8).

Why are Paul's words "all" (2 Tim. 4:8) and "everyone" (Eph. 6:8) encouraging? _____

_____

_____

_____

_____

_____

Randy Alcorn's book, *Heaven*, contains additional material not included in this *Masterwork* study. If you would like to read and study his book in greater detail, you can obtain your own copy of *Heaven* by visiting the LifeWay Christian Store serving you, or by calling 1-800-458-2772.

It won't be just a select few rewarded with positions of leadership.

Should we be excited that God will reward us by making us rulers in His kingdom? Absolutely. Jesus said, "Rejoice and be glad, because great is your reward in heaven" (Matt. 5:12).

God will choose who reigns as kings, and I think some great surprises are in store for us.

Look around you to see the meek and the humble. They may include street sweepers, locksmith's assistants, bus drivers, or stay-at-home moms who spend their days changing diapers, doing laundry, packing lunches, drying tears, and driving carpools for God.

I once gave one of my books to a delightful hotel bellman. I discovered he was a committed Christian. He said he'd been praying for our group, which was holding a conference at the hotel. Later, I gave him a little gift, a rough wooden cross. He seemed stunned, overwhelmed. With tears in his eyes he said, "You didn't need to do that. I'm only a bellman." The moment he said it, I realized that this brother had spent his life serving. It will likely be someone like him that I'll have the privilege of serving under in God's kingdom. He was "only a bellman" who spoke with warmth and love, who served, who quietly prayed in the background for the success of a conference in his hotel. I saw Jesus in that bellman, and there was no "only" about him.

Who will be the kings of the New Earth? I think that bellman will be one of them. And I'll be honored to carry his bags.

1. Wayne Grudem, *Systematic Theology: An Introduction to Biblical Doctrine* (Grand Rapids: Zondervan, 1994), 1158–1164.

LEADER GUIDE

To the Leader
Contact participants, prospects, and learners who have been absent lately and invite them to join you next week as you begin your study of *10 Choices* by James MacDonald..

During the Session

1. Ask participants to assume they have been asked to write a comprehensive report about another nation. Ask: *What kinds of information about that nation would you include in your report? Why is it, when we think of God's kingdom, we often think only of the King and His subjects and leave out the land, culture, and form of government?* Declare that God's promise has always emphasized managing land. The first thing God promised Abraham was land he could live on and manage in ways that would honor God and bless all the peoples of the world (Gen. 12:1-7). Read Galatians 3:29. Declare that believers won't just inherit the kingdom, but responsibilities within that kingdom.

2. Ask learners to open their Bibles to Revelation 5. Invite someone to read verse 1. Encourage learners to search Day One and state the significance of the scroll and the seven seals. Ask: *How are you comforted by the fact this scroll is in God's right hand?* (God is in control of history.) Discuss the first activity of Day One (p. 158). John was overwhelmed that God's final action in history couldn't move forward because no one was worthy. Determine why no one was worthy. Declare that just when it seems all hope was lost, hope entered the picture. Ask someone to read Revelation 5:5-9. Determine why Christ was worthy. State: *The Lion chose to become a Lamb and pay the price to reverse the curse on the earth.* Complete the second activity of Day One (p. 158). Analyze what it means for Christ's followers to be made a kingdom and priests. (They will share in God's rule and have complete access to God.) ☊

3. Allow participants to share how they feel about the concept of ruling with Christ. Declare that even if this seems a foreign concept we cannot disregard what Scripture says. Discuss the first two activities of Day Two (pp. 159,160). Analyze what a crown signifies in human terms. Ask: *Do you believe Christ's followers receive a crown? What does that crown signify?* Ask volunteers to read the printed verses from Revelation 2–5 in Day Two (p. 160). Discuss the two bolded questions following those verses (p. 161).

4. Declare that the crown—the rule—is a reward. Complete the first activities in Day Four (p. 163) and Day Five (p. 165). Ask: *Why might ruling not be some people's idea of a heavenly reward?* Declare that we must accept that it's God's idea. Because we're in His family, we participate in the family business of ruling the universe not as a grudging child who'd rather be doing something else but because it's a joy and privilege. Ask: *What do you consider a rewarding day—to sit around bored and do nothing or put in an honest day's work and accomplish something? Why? Imagine having leadership responsibilities over a creation untouched by sin and possessing full competence, energy, health, and time. Would you consider those responsibilities a privilege or drag? Why?* Declare that our service in Heaven won't just bring God glory, it will bring us joy. Invite responses to the second activity of Day Three (p. 163). Ask: *Do you think our service for God now influences how we'll serve in Heaven? How?* (Use the remarks and Luke 14:11 and 16:10 printed in Day Three to add to this discussion.) ◑

5. Request someone read the quote in the margin of Day Four (p. 164). Ask: *How is Christ preparing us now for leadership in the future? How might you handle heartaches and disappointments on this earth differently if you recognized God was using those to groom you for leadership on the new earth? Whom do you think will receive the positions of greatest leadership in the eternal Heaven?* Relate the closing story of Day Five.

6. Remind participants of the story from the week of October 16 (p. 84) about the pastor who dreaded going to Heaven because of all that "endless tedium. To float around in the clouds with nothing to do but strum a harp … it's all so terribly boring." Ask: *Is that going to be true of Heaven? Why?* Randy Alcorn declared: "Satan need not convince us that Heaven doesn't exist. He need only convince us that Heaven is a place of boring, unearthly existence" (p. 85). Ask: *How has this entire seven-week study of Heaven convinced you otherwise?* Close in prayer, thanking God for an eternally fulfilling and exciting home in Heaven. ◑